MEN LOVING MEN

MEN LOVING MEN

A Gay Sex Guide and Consciousness Book

Mitch Walker

Photographs by Franco/Ram Studios
Drawings by Bill Warrick

Gay Sunshine Press
San Francisco

Library of Congress Cataloging in Publication data:

Walker, Mitch, 1951–
    Men loving men : a gay sex guide and consciousness book

    Includes bibliographical references
    1. Homosexuality, Male.   2. Sexual intercourse.
I. Title
HQ76.W27   301.41'5   76-30587
ISBN 0-917342-52-6

ACKNOWLEDGMENTS

    Grateful acknowledgment is made to the following for permission to reprint from previously copyrighted material: Les Editions Nagel, for excerpts from *Sarv e' Naz, An Essay on Love and the Representation of Erotic Themes in Ancient Iran* by R. Surieu, copyright © 1967 by Nagel Publishers, Geneva; Les Editions Nagel, for the photos of *satyr, ephebe and pais*, and *scene from an orgy* in *Eros Kalos, Essay on Erotic Elements in Greek Art* by J. Marcade, copyright © 1962 by Nagel Publishers; Hawthorn Books, Inc., for the excerpts from *Homosexual Behavior Among Males* by W. Churchill, copyright © 1967 by Wainwright Churchill, all rights reserved; Harper and Row Publishers, Inc., for excerpts from *Patterns of Sexual Behavior* by C. Ford and F. Beach, copyright, 1951 by Clellan Stearns Ford and Frank Ambrose Beach, all rights reserved; G. P. Putnam's Sons for the drawings *from the Catamites' Scroll* in *Erotic Art of the East, The Sexual Theme in Oriental Painting and Sculpture* by P. Rawson, copyright © 1968 by Philip Rawson; G. P. Putnam's Sons for the woodcut *Twentieth Century Study in Erotic Art of the West* by R. Melville, copyright © Robert Melville 1973; W. W. Norton and Company, Inc., for excerpts from *Sexuality and Homosexuality, a New View* by A. Karlen, copyright © 1971 by Arno Karlen; Grove Press, Inc., for excerpts from *The Other Face of Love* by R. de Becker, copyright © 1969 by Neville Spearman Ltd.; Grove Press for the engraving *three soldiers* in *Sixty Erotic Engravings from Juliette*, copyright © 1969 by Grove Press.
    Every effort has been made to locate the copyright owners of the material quoted in the text. Omissions brought to our attention will be credited in subsequent printings.

Gay Sunshine Press
P.O. Box 410690
San Francisco, CA 94141
Send $1 for catalogue of books available.

Table of Contents

△

All photos of models by Franco/Ram Studios,
   San Francisco.
Drawings by Bill Warrick.
All captions on model photos by Winston Leyland.

AUTHOR'S PREFACE TO
SECOND EDITION

Seventeen years have passed since *Men Loving Men* first appeared. Much has changed during that time, yet the need to validate gay feelings is just as great today. Despite our growth as a social and political movement, gay desires for sex, love and relationships are still challenged by vicious homophobia and now, AIDS. A new puritanism stalks the land, along with a powerful reactionary Right utterly opposed to gay love.

This is the challenge facing those who seek to fulfill their gayness today. For people just coming out, the need for support is especially acute.

Therefore I'm glad that with this new revised edition, *Men Loving Men* will again be available to those who seek better self-understanding. In these pages you'll find a humane, factually based, supportive exploration of gay male sexuality, its history, practical mechanics, and relationship to valuable qualities such as love, honesty, self-realization and sacred spirit. Keep in mind, though, that the text references its own era.

The book's candid, personal tone arises from an era of youthful exuberance that still befits the innocent nature of Eternal Eros, that reflects the post-Stonewall surge to reclaim our bodies and our histories, our sex and our culture from a sea of bigotry and ignorance. This tone is still of value, but it must be tempered nowadays by caution about AIDS. For this new edition of *Men Loving Men* I have completely revised and updated the Gay Health chapter. To provide further guidance, we are also reprinting the current safe sex guidelines by the Bay Area Physicians for Human Rights (see page 37). The publisher and I urge you to be as safe as possible sexually, always use a latex condom when fucking, and get more information if you're not sure about something. This present edition also includes thirty-eight sensual new photographs by San Francisco's Franco/Ram Studios.

Now more than ever it's vital to honor and fulfill our sexuality, our capacity for love, and our spiritual potential. To me, these are not separate dimensions, but eternally one and the same. Especially in a time of catastrophe and challenge, to fully be all that we can be alone satisfies the urge to live and create, draws out our finest capabilities. Within gayness resides a profound Spirit, a giftedness desperately needed by our dysfunctional society as well as by the entire world. We live in an age of great possibilities. Therefore, I dedicate this second edition of *Men Loving Men* to gay youth, to full gay liberation, to the future. May these pages empower you to reach for your best and deepest dreams.

—*Mitch Walker,*
Hollywood, California

1

LOVING MEN, AN INTRODUCTION

Homosexuality is as old as humanity itself.

—Goethe

LOVING MEN,
AN INTRODUCTION

I want to tell you how I came to write this book and what it is about.

One sunny day while walking on Telegraph Avenue in Berkeley, I thought I'd go and browse in a bookstore for a while. On a shelf I saw a large-sized book titled *The Joy of Sex* by Alex Comfort, a book I'd never noticed before. I thought to myself, "Maybe this is a new kind of sex guide that will speak to *me*, about *my* needs and interests." So, full of hopeful fantasies, I flipped through the pages. I saw all the lovely drawings of a man and a woman together. I read some of the entries, about panties and rubbers and so on. I looked in the table of contents. Nothing there about my needs. I looked in the index—one entry under "bisexuality." Alex thought there was "nothing wrong with it" and to not get upset if you were at an orgy and someone of your sex wanted to make it with you. So that was the joy of sex!

My immediate reaction was that the cover title was very misleading. Not only was I disappointed, but sad and angry too. I wanted to read about loving, touching and hugging men. Why did writers like Comfort pretend my kind of love didn't exist, wasn't even worth talking about? Once a friend and I were having sex and he tried to fuck me in the ass. It hurt; I got scared. Afterwards, I felt I was really inadequate. I thought, "Everyone else knows what to do and has a super time, but I just get confused." There were sex guides for womenandmen—that was normal—but none for me.

So right then and there, I decided to write something for those who always got ignored, to give some support and guidance about men loving men. I read many books: sex guides, history books, medical books. I talked to doctors, psychologists, sexologists. I did "field research" and enlisted the help of "research assistants" to learn more about my own body and pleasures; and I talked to many friends and acquaintances about how they enjoyed sex, love, and touching with others. And here is the result, for me and you, who are men who want to love other men.

In the following pages, I will try to explain, in a simple and clear way, how one, two, and more males can share genital pleasures, the various styles and positions, and methods you can use to get into them. This book is complete; it tells of all the basic sexual techniques. Yet I give the information to you as possibility, as potential ways for you to go. For I'm first and foremost concerned with you doing what's good for you, being satisfied, having pleasure, growth, relaxation, centering, in being yourself.

As natural beings, we already have within us understanding of all types of sexual and sensual sharing. To realize this requires a good consciousness, being aware and understanding of yourself and your surroundings, a frame of mind at once positive, relaxed, joyful, and willing to explore, to be real and human. To be weak at times. This consciousness can't be forced or trained; it can only be awakened in a gentle manner. This is what I'm aiming for, to stimulate this consciousness in you, not just to say how you move this and that in the correct ways, but to ask you to unlock the understanding in yourself, to tease out what wants to express itself, for then you will be most pleased and pleasing. We tend to seek outside ourselves for the knowledge and assurance to be who we are, and do what we want. While describing how to do something, I also try to pique your curiosity about unravelling *your* secrets. The light inside shines bright, deep and warm—we feel it as beauty and strength.

So, I'm not just concerned with the mechanics of sex, with expertise, but also with its goodness for us as sensitive, growing people. Most of these pages are about sexual sharing, but I'm using sex as the ground floor to a large house, and it takes a clear diagram from which to build firm walls and attractive rooms. With many of us, sex is the socially easiest way to touch others and begin to be close with them. Thus, sex contains the introduction to other intimate and varied needs, feelings, and desires. I'm not saying this is a good or bad way to go about things—rather, I merely accept that this is how many people try to meet and grow with others. Therefore by first demystifying sex between men I can help clear the path for some of us, and point towards a few of those other needs.

Sex can't happen without touch. Touch is warm and caring: these lead to many feelings in us, to love. In this way, all is one, and like a gem or a living tree, indivisible. That's why I couldn't have made just a techniques manual. That's why this is a sex guide *and* a consciousness book, a growing book.

Thus, the book (even when it's speaking in dry words about sex techniques) is about many things. About touching, with your penis, with your finger tips, your heart, with curiosity, warmth. About suggestions, the maybe's, wanting to expand awareness and enjoyment. Paths to walk down, thirsts to quench. About pleasures, an invitation to growth, excitement, love, satisfaction, whatever. The good consciousness I spoke of before involves this feeling: sex is fun. That's why I do it, it feels nice. And sexual experiences that are enjoyable and satisfying confirm the person, their meaning, substance, self.

Part of pleasure is always light, humorous. So this is also a book about smiling. About laughing, especially at yourself in a good-natured way. For humor will grease your explorations, sweeten your mistakes, and fill your ecstacy with joy. Humor is unfailing, because sex is playful, "easily compared to the games of children and puppies," as the psychologist Abraham Maslow said.

A healthy dose of humor is indispensable, especially when dealing with problems (because it unlocks the latch of sorrow). Laugh at your mistakes, at your absurd fears and dreads, and you'll walk through the door—coming too soon, can't get it up? It's never catastrophic, you won't get castrated. Rather, you'll feel safer, more yourself. Then sexual experience/expression becomes fuller, deeper—personable, intimately unique to the person and the setting, and free of plastic expectations. It becomes comfortable, loose, refreshing. Needs blend together, as they will, in whatever ways are good at the time: you start, stop, get hotter, talk, cuddle, race, relax, laugh, as you feel good doing. You may or may not have orgasm at all. You become liquid; you flow; you are free.

I frown on all the deceptions sex can become—performance, power, ego, and so on. These games are defenses against being hurt, but are usually harmful. Also I'm down on avoidance: many people are hungry for care and affection and use sex as a substitute. Better to skip all these games and be honest: sex is pleasure through genital excitement. It can become a high form of love, but not a substitute. If you want sex, just say so. If you want touch, ask for it—get what you need, by being honest and direct.

And so also, because I'm honest, this is a book about bad things as well as good, for there is no good without bad. Where there is pleasure, there is often sorrow, too. I'd be fooling myself and you, if I didn't say this, and pretended that sex is the greatest heaven on earth and each of us an angel—that sex is full of eternal bliss and all-consuming satisfactions. We live in a world full of pain and suffering, of exploitation, starvation, of horrible injustices. It gets so bad that many of us just want to escape, pop pills all the time, hide in our televisions, in our beds, in our cocks and cunts. Sometimes I get so lonely and afraid, I can't be with anyone. Often, especially for many months a while back, I wanted just to be hugged, to be held, to be with a warm friend. I have experienced some of my deepest times this way, being weak, being comforted, touching out and being touched without any intentions, any goals, any movement. I've shared pain as well as joy in this way, and felt the healing power of hands, the free giving of care, and I've freely given care like this too.

Thus, in all these ways I've mentioned above, this is a book for people who want to be themselves. Being yourself may not be such an easy thing—our society has a passion for telling/making/forcing us to be what we should be. From birth, and in every way, they indoctrinate us into what's good for us and what's bad, to program our lives and loves.

I bet your parents told you that little boys don't cry, and little girls don't act rough. In this way they were trying to shape your idea of sex role, who a man and a woman are, and how they should be and act. For a man, it was especially important to put on a show of being rough, tough, competent, a leader, cold, powerful in pushing other men around and proving sexual prowess with women. It was very bad to fail at this. Worst of all was for a man to touch and love another man, to be tender together. Think of it—two men, tall, hairy, kissing each other, leaning on each other, gazing into each other's eyes.

So finally, this is a book about love feelings, some of what they are, some ways to grow into them. Many of us name this "gay love," so we can call it our own. This gayness is a self-made choice, your decision to do what's good for you sexually, sensually, emotionally, lovingly, and so on. It's perhaps the joy to love those of your sex, to want to hold them in your arms, to be there. It's an energy coming from within, to celebrate yourself. It is respect.

To be gay is not to be a homosexual. "Homosexuality" is a label put on some of us by ill-meaning scientists; it usually means a sex preference, and absolutely so. Gayness goes infinitely beyond sex, and may not include it at all. Each is gay in her/his own way—it is a perspective, a flowering.

There is a bond between us, who have these desires, which is deep and beautiful. We *know* each other, can share feelings others would never understand. A common suffering, a common wish. We can harness this for our good, for together we can do what we could not do separately. So gay is being *with us:* we are all kin, trying to build a kind of family, a sense of community, old and young, male and female. In this way we confirm others' gayness. And it feels good.

This warmth blossoms in us as we realize our true nature. Uncovering this can be difficult, for our society has tried to destroy all knowledge of gay feelings, people, culture, and growth. We have been invisible. It is important now to make all aspects of gayness (whether you choose to use this label or not) as visible as possible, to take back the knowledge we need to be ourselves.

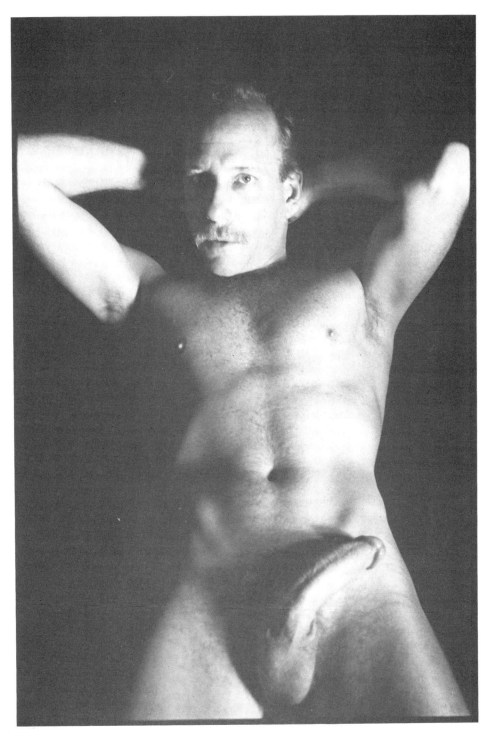

Photo © Franco/Ram Studios, San Francisco, 1994. All the subsequent model photos in this book are by the same photographer.

That's why I'm writing this book. We learn about gay sex in alley-ways, in whispers, sometimes confused, sometimes scared. Now is the time to say, here are some of the things you can do, and how to do them—so you will know what you are capable of. To demystify—in this way only can we regain control over ourselves.

We can learn much from others about gayness, from our friends and from our ancestors. We are hardly the first to describe and praise gay love and sex—there is a great history of gayness among peoples, its prevalence and variety since the dawn of time. This is also a part of us, and so throughout the book, sections are devoted to gay history. Because it was so comforting and instructive for me to know about this, I'd like to spend some time here presenting the depth of gayness, by way of introduction.

I will give brief pictures, vignettes, of aspects of gayness in different species and cultures, as expressed by scholars and the peoples of these cultures. I feel my comments would add little to what has already been said, so I am deleting any commentary and just presenting sets of quotations. This material is mainly on male gayness, since I'm not qualified to speak on the history of women.

Notes at the end of this book document each of the following quotes which are all taken from books by modern scholars unless otherwise indicated.

Male Gayness in Western Civilization

The oldest literary testimony hitherto known dates back more than 4,500 years, and is to be found in an Egyptian papyrus which proves not only that paederasty was at that time widespread in Egypt but also that it was presumed to exist among the gods as a matter of course.[1]

o   o   o

With the exception of the Hebrews and possibly though not certainly the Assyrians, we can find no evidence that the ancient peoples of the Mediterranean and Near East ever attempted to suppress the practice of homosexual love . . .[2]

o   o   o

The ancient Jews in pre-Exile time [Babylonian Exile, about 700 B.C.] did not condemn homosexual practices.[3]

o   o   o

Among the Hittites, who possessed the most ancient civilization of Asia Minor, legal marriage existed between men and boys . . .[4]

o   o   o

"Bad news, my lord prince! I have very bad news for you, I am sorry to say. Patroclos is dead, they are fighting for his body . . ."

Sorrow fell on Achilles like a cloud. He swept up the dust with both hands, and poured it over his head and smirched his handsome face, till the black dirt stained his fragrant tunic. He tore his hair and fell flat in the dust, grand in his grandeur. . . . Antilochos had taken the hands of Achilles and stood weeping beside him, while he moaned heavily; for he feared Achilles might put the steel to his own throat.[5]

—*The Iliad,* as told by Homer, ca. 850 B.C.

o   o   o

The Story of the Birth of Democracy:

"Harmodius was then a most beautiful young man in the flower of his youth, and was loved and possessed by Aristogiton, a citizen who belonged to the middle class. Harmodius was approached, though without success, by Hipparchus, the son of Pisistratus [the old dictator of Athens], and he told Aristogiton of this, who, being in love as he was, was greatly upset and was afraid that Hipparchus, with all his power, might take Harmodius by force. He therefore began at once, so far as he could in his position, to plot to overthrow the dictatorship . . .

"When the day of the festival came . . . Harmodius and Aristogiton had their daggers ready and were preparing to take action when they saw one of their fellow-conspirators talking in a friendly manner with Hippias [brother of Hipparchus]. . . . They then became frightened, thinking that the plot had been betrayed and that they were on the very point of being arrested. . . . So they rushed inside the gates just as they were, came upon Hipparchus by the Leocorium, and immediately fell upon him without a thought for their own safety, but acting entirely under the impulse of rage. . . . So they struck him down and killed him."[6]

—as told by Thucydides the Greek historian (ca. 471–400 B.C.)

o   o   o

Ephebe and pais. Makron. An Attic cup.
Museum of Munich

To be fond of good-looking and well-behaved young people is a
natural tendency of all sensitive and liberal minds.[7]
— Aeschines the Athenian orator (389–314 B.C.)

      °   °   °

. . . our basic moral laws and ethics were originally propounded by
men who practiced homosexuality in their youth—such as Solon, Socrates, Plato, and Aristotle. Our ideal of beauty in architecture and

sculpture were delineated by men like Phidias, whose love for a handsome youth was carved in marble for everyone to see. The forms of dramatic writing employed today were first used by Sophocles, Euripides, and Aristophanes—all of whom had homosexual attachments at one time or another.

The earliest military heroes, whose exploits are still read with admiration, were men like Alexander, Achilles, and Epaminondas, all of whose homosexual connections are matters of record. Even the mythical hero Hercules, the fabled strongest and bravest man in the world, had his immortal homosexual companion—Iolaus, his chariot-driver.

Thus, paradoxically, our puritanically-oriented Western civilization and morality seem to have been built upon a solid rock of homosexuality![8]

◦   ◦   ◦

Homosexuality was not only prevalent and uncensored in the Roman civilization but the love of young men was highly esteemed. It was not until the time of Constantine and Justinian, when Christianity, introducing an ancient Hebraic moral code, was made the official religion of Roman government that homosexuality was in any way condemned.[9]

◦   ◦   ◦

But it is not the same thing, I want a fig not an orange, and you must know theirs is a fig, yours an orange; Look! a matron, a woman like you, must know what belongs to her. Leave to boys what is theirs, and do you make the best of what is yours.[10]
    —Valerius Martial the Roman epigrammatist (ca. 40–102 A.D.)

◦   ◦   ◦

The following Roman emperors were thought to have had homosexual experiences: Caesar (d. 44 B.C.), Augustus (d. A.D. 14), Tiberius (d. 37), Caligula (41), Claudius (54), Nero (68), Galba (69), Otho (69), Vitellius (69), Titus (81), Domitian (96), Nerva (98), Trajan (117), Hadrian (138), Commodus (192), Elagabalus (222), Theodosius II of the East (450), Valentinian III of the West (455).[11]

◦   ◦   ◦

Inversion has always been easy to trace in Germany. Ammianus Marcellinus bears witness to its prevalence among some German tribes in later Roman days. . . . In early Teutonic days there was little or no

19

trace of any punishment for homosexual practice. This, according to Herman Michaelis, appeared after the Church had gained power among the West Goths. . . . In England . . . it is doubtful whether it has been less prevalent than in Germany.[12]

o   o   o

A great many popes, kings, and other high royalty of medieval and modern Europe were thought to have had some homosexual leanings, including Richard I (Lion Hearted) of England (d. 1199), Edward II of England (1327), Henry IV of Castile (1474), James I of England (1625), Louis XIII of France (1643) and Frederick II (the Great) of Prussia (1786).[13]

o   o   o

But homosexuality was clearly commonplace in urban Italy, [and] present in France [during the Renaissance—during the fifteenth and sixteenth centuries].[14]

o   o   o

Throughout life he [Leonardo da Vinci: 1452–1519] loved to surround himself with beautiful youths and his pupils were more remarkable for their attractive appearance than for their skill.[15]

o   o   o

All them that love not tobacco and boys are fooles.[16]
        —attributed to the poet Christopher Marlowe (1564–1593)

o   o   o

Antinous, so named because, like Hadrian's favorite, he had, together with the world's prettiest prick, its most voluptuous ass, and that is exceedingly rare. Antinoüs wielded a device measuring eight inches in circumference and twelve in length. He was thirty and had a face worthy of his other features.[17]
        —The Marquis de Sade (1740–1814), The 120 Days of Sodom, 1785

o   o   o

In the eighteenth century there was a great craze for English imitations of Anacreon [an ancient Greek poet who wrote many homosexual

20

love poems], and one such led to a popular song, "Anacreon in Heaven," which in due course furnished the tune for the American national anthem.[18]

o   o   o

Few people today recognize the part homosexuality played in the life of the early American male. . . . Frontier-life occupations isolated men from women for long periods. . . . homosexuality was largely taken for granted.[19]

o   o   o

I HEAR it was charged against me, that I sought to destroy institutions,
But really I am neither for nor against institutions,
(What indeed have I in common with them? or what with the
     destruction of them?)
Only I will establish in the Mannahatta and in every city of these
     States inland and seaboard,
And in the fields and woods, and above every keel little or large that
     dents the water,
Without edifices or rules or trustees or any argument,
The institution of the dear love of comrades.[20]
                       —Walt Whitman (1819–1892)

o   o   o

Their world, he said, was organized, with its own words, customs and traditions, its churches, meeting places, cafes and streets . . .[21]
        —anonymous letter to Havelock Ellis, end of 19th century

o   o   o

At least 37 per cent of the male population [of the U.S.] has some homosexual experience between the beginning of adolescence and old age. . . . Some of these persons have but a single experience, and some of them have much more or even a lifetime of experience, but all of them have at least some experience to the point of orgasm.

These figures are, of course, higher than any which have previously been estimated; but as already shown (Chapter 4) they must be understatements if they are anything other than the fact.[22]

—Alfred Kinsey and others, *Sexual Behavior in the Human Male,* 1948

Male Gayness in Middle Eastern and Indian Cultures

Throughout the Orient, and in all Oriental cultures, homosexual practices have been recognized and held in honor, at times, above heterosexual love.[23]

o   o   o

Turks were "generally addicted, besides all their sensuall and incestuous lusts, unto Sodomy, which they account as a daynty to digest all their other libidinous pleasures."[24]
—William Lithgow, Scotch traveller, about 1620

o   o   o

A boy of twice ten is fit for a king![25]
—*The Thousand and One Nights*

o   o   o

The Persians of past centuries rated highly the pleasures to be had from the enjoyment of handsome boys: a pleasure which in their eyes seemed entirely natural. . . . it is clear that true love—*l'amour de coeur*—was not, as a rule, inspired by a woman, but by some handsome youth.[26]

o   o   o

His curls in disarray, perspiring, laughing, drunk,
His garments torn, singing a poem, his glass in his hand,
With challenging eye and enchanting mouth,
He came, last night at midnight, and sat beside my couch;
Then bent his head and whispered in my ear, in accents sad:
'O my erstwhile loved one, art thou asleep?'
The lover to whom such wine as this is offered in the dawn
Turns heretic in love unless he becomes a worshipper of wine.[27]
—Hafiz (d. 1389)

o   o   o

Sa'di, the "Persian moralist" begins one of his tales, "A certain learned man fell in love with a beautiful *son* of a blacksmith," which Gladwin, translating for the general, necessarily changed to "Daughter."[28]
—Sir Richard Burton (1821–1890)

o   o   o

The American street corner with its collection of scrutinizers of passing girls finds its historical counterpart in the open Mohammedan geh-weh (coffee house), where men utterly ignored the passing doe-eyed lass. Women were abundant and cheap, but the provocative, rump-wriggling lad was a treasure, and men puffed and snorted, devouring with glaring eyes any willow-branch of a lad who quivered by.[29]

o   o   o

In Shiraz, an eminent *mujtahid* (spiritual director of the Sheeah sect) was suddenly approached by one of his colleagues. "There is a question I would fain address to thine Eminence," he said, hesitant and pensive, "but I lack the daring to do so."

"Ask, and fear not!"

"Then it is this, O Mujtahid! Figure thee in a garden of roses and hyacinths, with the evening breeze waving the cyprus heads, a fair youth of twenty sitting by thy side, and the assurance of perfect privacy. What, prithee, would be the result?"

The theologian grinned, then scowled out, and wringing his fists and beating his ears, hastened away. "Almighty God defend me from such temptation!"[30]

—A Persian story

o   o   o

Three out of five Arabs preferred the sexual service of a handsome young beardless lad or a serviceable eunuch to that of any beautiful woman.[31]

o   o   o

The atheistic or shamanistic Turanians, Cossacks, and Bulgars (whence the word *bugger*), Huns, Tartars, Mongols, Kurds, Turkomans, Yakuts, many of them nomadic brigands and savage warriors, were dubbed *hurfooshees* (scoundrels) by civilized Asia because of their flagrant sodomy.[32]

o   o   o

Yet the average Hindoo was generally open-minded toward *gaundh-ruttee* (anal coition) because of Lord Shiva, the celestial embodiment of worldly vice, who was said to have copulated with the *raukshehs*, Vishnu, and others of the gods. Shiva was also solemnly masturbated by Agnee the Fire-Lord . . .[33]

o   o   o

From the Catamites' Scroll(Chigo no Soshi), dated 1321. Sambo-in temple, Daigo, Japan. The earliest example of an actual erotic scroll in Heian court style known to survive, preserved in a temple

Formation of homosexual camaraderie to maintain martial strength and unity can be found among the Sikhs, Rajpoots, Mahrattas, Pathans (*Pudhauns*), the Ghilzyes, Dorranee Afghans, and hill frontiersmen of northern India.[34]

Male Gayness in the Far East

In the Far East it is impossible to find any condemnation of homosexuality by the religions which have taken root there.[35]

°   °   °

The commission of this detestable and unnatural act is attended with so little shame, or feelings of delicacy, that many of the first officers of the state seemed to make no hesitation in publically avowing it. Each of these officers is constantly attended by his pipe-bearer, who is generally a handsome boy from fourteen to eighteen years of age, and is always well dressed.[36]

—Sir John Barrow, *Travels in China*, 1806

o   o   o

In ancient China this feeling [of friendship] gave rise to a curious custom, which was related both to homosexual marriage and adoption contracts—that of 'dry relationships.' Two friends who wanted to seal their friendship and ensure for it some kind of social recognition could declare themselves 'dry brothers.' . . . They were solemnized before witnesses and had the same validity as the most formal deed in writing.[37]

o   o   o

All the priests and some of the nobility are strongly attached to unnatural lusts; they do not make any sin of this propensity, and neither feel shame or remorse on account of it.[38]

—Hagenaar and Frans Caron visiting Japan, about 1630

o   o   o

As in Greece, it was honorable at the time of the Samurai to have a young boy as one's lover, and despicable never to have had one.[39]

o   o   o

Hayemon continued to consider Mondo as his young lover. He arranged his thin hair with his own hands in the style of a page's hair, using much perfumed oil. Mondo's brow was like that of a woman, and he took great care of his person; he polished his nails with aromatic wood, and shaved himself carefully. There is no doubt that these two old men continued their amorous encounters up to an advanced age.[40]

—Saikaku Ihara (1641–1693), *Comrade Loves of the Samurai*

o   o   o

That homosexual love was never abandoned by the Japanese in modern times may be seen in the fact that teahouses with male *geishas* still existed in Japan until the end of the Second World War, when they were suppressed by the American occupation forces.[41]

Dance to the Berdash. George Catlin, 1841

Male Gayness Among "Primitive" Cultures

In forty-nine (sixty-four per cent) of the seventy-six societies other than our own for which information is available, homosexual activities of one sort or another are considered normal and socially acceptable for certain members of the community.[42]

      o   o   o

The most common form of institutionalized homosexuality is the *berdache,* or transvestite.[43]

      o   o   o

Exclusive or near-exclusive homosexuality appears to be more rare in preliterate societies than in the more complex civilizations. . . . But actual incidence rates vary greatly between societies, ranging for males from nearly 100 percent to zero.[44]

      o   o   o

Among the tribes found near Lake Chad (in Africa) there are groups of homosexual nomads who, in the northern part of the area, go from town to town in order to abandon themselves to prostitution, and who are feted like royalty everywhere.[45]

o   o   o

In Ramree Island, off the coast of Burma, some sorcerers adopt women's dress, become the "husband" of a colleague, and then bring him a woman as a "second wife," with whom both men cohabit. . . . Ritual transformation [by the shaman] into a woman also occurs among the Kamchadal, the Asiatic Eskimo, and the Koryak . . .[and also] in Indonesia (the *manangbali* of the Sea Dyak), in South America (Patagonians and Araucanians), and among certain North American tribes (Arapaho, Cheyenne, Ute, etc.).[46]

o   o   o

Among 225 American Indian tribes, 53% accepted male homosexuality, again to at least a limited degree . . .[47]

o   o   o

The American Indians do not make Plato's high moral claims for homosexuality, but homosexuals are often regarded as exceptionally able.[48]

Homosexual Behavior Among Animals

[Homosexual activity] occurs in every type of animal that has been carefully studied. [49]

o   o   o

Two male porpoises that were studied for several months formed a close attachment to each other. One member of the pair was removed from the tank for three weeks. The reactions of the two males upon their reunion were described in the following quotation:

"No doubt could exist that the two recognized each other, and for several hours they swam side by side rushing frenziedly through the water, and on several occasions they leaped completely out of the water. For several days, the two males were inseparable and neither paid any attention to the female. This was in courting season, and at other times the two males seemed bent only on preventing the other's copulation with the female."[50]

Gayness, as sex and love, as a way to be, is universal, honored in one or more variations among Nature, through history and in the majority of human cultures. There is a vital force in it which cannot be killed or suppressed. Its natural, essential life-energy will blossom within even the most hostile environments, such as our western Christian society. Almost two thousand years of the most vitriolic suppression and condemnation have not rooted it out of us—and now that condemnation itself begins to wither.

Gay people—those of us who have oriented ourselves by this unique essence—have been struggling ever since oppression started, to be free to do as we chose. And people have been organizing gay rights groups for over a hundred years! Slowly but surely we have made headway; there have been many illustrious deeds and names in this struggle, Walt Whitman, John Addington Symonds, Magnus Hirschfeld, Radcliffe Hall, André Gide, Gertrude Stein, Oscar Wilde, to name but a few. We are all that much closer to freedom because of those who have gone before. Millions before you have held other men's hands, kissed them, and expressed the joys and depths of gay feelings.

To cultivate your gay feelings and gayness, as *your* needs and potential define, to say "This is good—let it grow!" is to reach inward to the best, warmest, most strong parts of yourself. If you have gayness, keeping it down and apart will only make you fragmented; letting it grow will make you whole.

Many people with gay feelings feel bad, as if that part of them were nasty or wrong, or their lives were condemned. Our society says nothing positive, and shows no way to grow. This can result in much isolation, and the pains of loneliness, blocking our needs for trust, warmth, caring, love, and sex. Our society tries to suffocate us, making us happy to grab a one-night stand, or slit our wrists.

I know what it's like to grow up alone, afraid of being discovered, guilty, lovestarved sick, no one to talk to, to comfort me, lost. I'd look at the other boys and know that I needed a friend, yet I never got the courage to reach out. I didn't know how. And later when I got into the cruising scene I became confused, gagging, hurting.

I feel that by providing this book I can help others avoid some of these troubles.

In all these pages I'm presenting information *and* opinion, from my point of view. Don't believe everything you read; check it out for yourself. Browse around and explore what you want. A person only grows by interacting with something and making it their own, in their own way. That's how I made this book, and I hope that's how you'll use it.

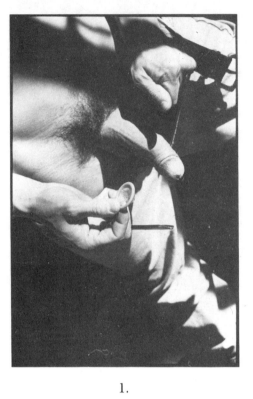

1.

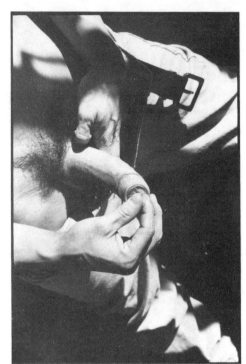

2.

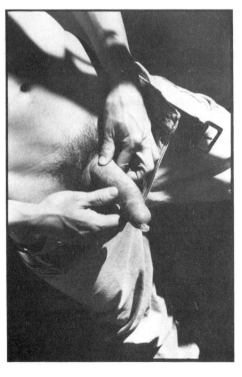

3.

4.

2

GAY HEALTH

How to Use a Condom

One of the nation's major gay health groups suggests the following method in using a condom. They emphasize that you should *always* use a latex condom for anal or vaginal sex:

1. Keep the cock free of grease.
2. Put a dab of lubricant inside the tip of the condom. This will increase sensitivity.
3. *Always* use a water based lubricant like KY. Lubricants made with oil (petroleum or vegetable) may damage the rubber.
4. Leaving a ½ inch space in the tip of the rubber as a reservoir, place the condom against the erect cock.
5. Squeeze out any air in the tip.
6. With the other hand unroll the rubber all the way to the base of the cock, smoothing out any excess air. If you are uncut, pull back the foreskin before covering the head with the rubber.
7. Hold on to the base of the condom while pulling out. Withdraw gently. *Use the condom only once.*

Many condoms are now made in both regular and extra large size, so keep supplies of both for safety and the comfort of your partner.

The Examination of the Herald. Aubrey Beardsley.
Drawing for *The Lysistrata of Aristophanes,* 1896

GAY HEALTH

It's very important these days to be health conscious, especially if your're thinking of having sex. There are many serious diseases that can be shared during sexual activities, diseases like gonorrhea, syphilis, hepatitis and AIDS. These are known as sexually transmitted diseases (STDs), and it's important to know how you can protect yourself and your friends against them.

The best protection comes from knowledge: knowing about the different kinds, their symptoms, the ways you can get them, and what to do to take care of yourself. Knowing how to stay healthy will protect your playful explorations in gay eros, enabling the work of gay liberation to blossom on and on. Mental and physical well being *as gay* is our birthright; empower yourself to take what's yours.

Acquired Immune Deficiency Syndrome (AIDS)

Of all the diseases spread through sex, Acquired Immune Deficiency Syndrome (AIDS) is by far the most deadly and terrifying. First noticed in 1979, the AIDS epidemic has since spread nationally and world-wide. In the U.S. alone, hundreds of thousands are already infected and many tens of thousands have died, mostly gay and bisexual men (though world-wide most infected people are heterosexual).

AIDS is caused by the Human Immunodeficiency Virus (HIV), which can be spread through the intimate exchange of blood or come. Blood is exchanged mainly by drug addicts sharing their needles, and come is exchanged primarily through fucking (both anal and vaginal), although cock sucking seems to have some risk factor also. HIV is not spread casually, so you can't get it from toilet seats, coughing, or used forks.

Once inside the body HIV acts as a silent parasite: it invades and sucks off the body's immune system, eventually disabling it. The immune system protects us from infections and diseases, and when it fails the body becomes vulnerable to a whole host of serious illnesses such as Kaposi's sarcoma and pneumocycstis pneumonia, referred to as opportunistic infections (OIs). When an HIV-positive person develops OIs and/or shows severe immunocompromise, he or she is diagnosed with AIDS.

HIV strangles the immune system gradually, and no symptoms may show for a long time, maybe even ten years or more. But eventually minor problems develop, such as persistent skin infections, swollen lymph nodes, fatigue, and, after further months or years, full-blown opportunists appear. These in turn wear the body down until death finally follows. There is currently no cure for this disease, yet people are learning how to make it more manageable, extending the quality and quantity of life.

The advent of antibody testing in the mid-80s has made it easy to identify and monitor infections from the start, and various interventions have been developed to slow the disease process and prevent OIs.

Therefore if there's any possibility you may be infected, it's important to get tested, and if you are positive, it's important to arrange for ongoing medical monitoring. Most large cities now have HIV-antibody testing sites, AIDS clinics and service groups, hotlines and so on that you can call for further information (also see below). There are also many excellent books now available about AIDS, risk-reduction and HIV-disease management.

From observing how people fall ill, doctors conclude that AIDS is not just a simple matter of getting the virus and then getting sick. Rather, additional factors influence disease progression, AIDS has *co-factors* in its development. One major co-factor as we have seen is time, while another is stress on the immune system. So one way you can help protect yourself from AIDS is to protect your body's immune system from stress. Major sources of stress include: repeated infections from STDs especially including HIV, recreational drug and alcohol abuse, poor nutrition, lack of sleep or exercise, and emotional and psychological stress.

Anxiety and other stressful feelings can have many causes, including fear of AIDS and trying to cope with the crisis. If you're experiencing difficulty making changes or handling feelings, don't feel you have to struggle alone. It's very important to talk about difficult emotions. For those with HIV, support organizations and groups are often available. There are also many gay counselors, psychologists and other professionals out there sensitive to gay needs today, and we want to be of help to you. I also encourage you to speak with friends and/or family.

In addition, there are various techniques that can aid in reducing stress and anxiety, such as aerobic exercise, meditation, yoga, and guided imagery. Participating in a "larger cause," such as political organizing or nonprofit volunteering, can also be quite helpful. To find out more, contact your nearest HIV service group, gay center, switchboard or alternate healing network and ask about services and resources (or write for a copy of the current National Edition of the *Gay Yellow Pages*, available for $13.95 postpaid from Renaissance House, Box 292, Village Station, New York, NY 10014, which contains addresses and phone numbers for health services and gay groups throughout the U.S. and Canada).

Since HIV is spread through come, it's important to follow risk-reduction guidelines, such as those by the Bay Area Physicians For Human Rights reprinted in this chapter. I urge you to be as safe as possible without compromising your integrity or growth, to help your partners also be safe, and to get more information or seek help if you're not sure.

In general, not engaging in insertive behaviors is safer than doing so, and if you do insert/get inserted, use a latex condom. Non-insertive activities like J/O, S/M, etc., are not as risky. Massage, cuddling and hugging are all perfectly safe. Kissing is probably safe under most circumstances. Another way to cut down on risk is to cut down on the number of different sex partners you're having. Also, it's a good idea to first get to know anyone you're thinking of having sex with. The Age of AIDS calls for brotherly concern. Before having sex find out a little about his background and attitude towards health, and tell him about yours. Doing this will encourage healthfulness and trust. It's vital for us all to be sensitive and open here, and talking about health concerns before getting it on is survival oriented.

You can do almost everything in this book in a safer way with a little extra awareness. Condoms can be eroticized. You can forgo a riskier type of activity in favor of deeper exploring in a safer area. Again, talking about it and getting input will help you find the way most nurturing and loving to yourself and your partners.

AIDS is challenging gay liberation to change and grow beyond its current limits, forcing us to discover if there's anything else to being gay besides how we suck and fuck. Historically gay men have thought of themselves as *homosexuals*, identity defined by sexual behavior. But this concept channeled post-Stonewall gay liberation too often into a rabbit-like frenzy of heartless humping and sucking, deluging us with STDs while neglecting deeper needs and potentials. I'm not talking about promiscuity per se but rather a narrowing of our humanity. Our creative erotic powers were shackled to a destructive myth, draining our vitality in the process.

Gays are not just homosexuals. We're carriers of a precious gift, we're an ancient *people* with a *spirit* and a *soul*. To nurture that faery soul and manifest that queer spirit in self and the world is what being gay is all about.

AIDS is daring us to grasp our fate, to chuck our mental conditioning, to consciously *come out inside*. Within you lies the *real* universe, the source of your gayness, and only liberating gay self there goes to the root of our challenge to survive and grow. Gay Spirit lives inside you, and it's the ongoing process of coming out inside that generates and feeds gay soul.

So the final AIDS risk-reduction guideline is: listen for wholeness calling you from your heart, then follow it down and in to its source. This will ask of you a descent into your own unconscious, an encounter with your shadow there, and a journeying on a quest. Nowadays we call this "inner work." But it's an archetypal way, individuation path of an ancient gay heritage as evolutionary change agents, as shamans and healers. Becoming gay has always been and always will be a spiritual process of inner initiation and unfolding, magically self-transformative, leading to queer treasures at a golden source.

A good way to begin inner work is by getting into gay-supportive psychotherapy. An additional way (if not already part of therapy), is to start a *dream journal*—a blank pad or notebook next to your bed where you can record any dreams you remember and the date you had them, writing down as much detail as possible. Then after keeping the journal awhile you'll be able to look back over your dreams, exploring for unfolding patterns, themes and meaning that engage the archetypal. And this exploration will be helped along a whole lot if you start telling your dreams to friends, and begin working on them with somebody experienced in entering the inner life consciously, for example someone well-versed in the dream amplification techniques of C. G. Jung. Jung was very interested in the encounter with the archetypes, which he called "individuation," and there are many good books available on Jungian psychology and dreamwork.

For true initiation in Gay Spirit, the way to reach the stars is by going down. Therapy, dreamwork and other methods to open the unconscious, when approached with a gay-positive attitude, can help you meet and grow with the deeper, transpersonal forces that exist inside you and then maybe they'll take you within the mysteries of gay love and transmutation. For more on transpersonal forces, see also the last chapter of this book. A new stage of gay liberation is upon us, and as we respond we will be birthing a needed future, both for ourselves and the world.

AIDS RISK REDUCTION GUIDELINES
FOR HEALTHIER SEX

As given by Bay Area Physicians for Human Rights

NO RISK: *Most of these activities involve only skin-to-skin contact, thereby avoiding exposure to blood, semen, and vaginal secretions. This assumes there are no breaks in the skin.* 1) **Social kissing** (dry). 2) **Body massage, hugging.** 3) **Body to body rubbing** (frottage). 4) **Light S&M** (without bruising or bleeding). 5) **Using one's own sex toys.** 6) **Mutual masturbation** (male or external female). Care should be taken to avoid exposing the partners to ejaculate or vaginal secretions. Seminal, vaginal and salivary fluids should not be used as lubricants.

LOW RISK: *In these activities small amounts of certain body fluids might be exchanged, or the protective barrier might break causing some risk.* 1) **Anal or vaginal intercourse with condom.** Studies have shown that HIV does not penetrate the condom in simulated intercourse. Risk is incurred if the condom breaks or if semen spills into the rectum or vagina. The risk is further reduced if one withdraws before climax. 2) **Fellatio interruptus** (sucking, stopping before climax). Pre-ejaculate fluid may contain HIV. Saliva or other natural protective barriers in the mouth may inactivate virus in pre-ejaculate fluid. Saliva may contain HIV in low concentration. The insertive partner should warn the receptive partner before climax to prevent exposure to a large volume of semen. If mouth or genital sores are present, risk is increased. Likewise, action which causes mouth or genital injury will increase risk. 3) **Fellatio with condom** (sucking with condom) Since HIV cannot penetrate an intact condom, risk in this practice is very low unless breakage occurs. 4) **Mouth-to-mouth kissing** (French kissing, wet kissing) Studies have shown that HIV is present in saliva in such low concentration that salivary exchange is unlikely to transmit the virus. Risk is increased if sores in the mouth or bleeding gums are present. 5) **Oral-vaginal or oral-anal contact with protective barrier.** e.g. a latex dam, obtainable through a local dental supply house, may be used. Do not reuse latex barrier, because sides of the barrier may be reversed inadvertently. 6) **Manual anal contact with glove** (manual anal (fisting) or manual vaginal (internal) contact with glove). If the glove does not break, virus transmission should not occur. However, significant trauma can still be inflicted on the rectal tissues leading to other medical problems, such as hemorrhage or bowel perforation. 7) **Manual vaginal contact with glove** (internal). See above.

MODERATE RISK: *These activities involve tissue trauma and/or exchange of body fluids which may transmit HIV or other sexually transmitted disease.* 1) **Fellatio** (sucking to climax). Semen may contain high concentrations of HIV and if absorbed through open sores in the mouth or digestive tract could pose risk. 2) **Oral-anal contact** (rimming). HIV may be contained in blood-contaminated feces or in the anal rectal lining. This practice also poses high risk of transmission of parasites and other gastrointestinal infections. 3) **Cunnilingus** (oral-vaginal contact). Vaginal secretions and menstrual blood have been shown to harbor HIV, thereby causing risk to the oral partner if open lesions are present in the mouth or digestive tract. 4) **Manual rectal contact** (fisting). Studies have indicated a direct association between fisting and HIV infection for both partners. This association may be due to concurrent use of recreational drugs, bleeding, pre-fisting semen exposure, or anal intercourse with ejaculation. 5) **Sharing sex toys.** 6) **Ingestion of urine.** HIV has not been shown to be transmitted via urine; however, other immunosuppressive agents or infections may be transmitted in this manner.

HIGH RISK: *These activities have been shown to transmit HIV.* 1) **Receptive anal intercourse without condom.** All studies imply that this activity carries the highest risk of transmitting HIV. The rectal lining is thinner than that of the vagina or the mouth thereby permitting ready absorption of the virus from semen or pre-ejaculate fluid to the blood stream. One laboratory study suggests that the virus may enter by direct contact with rectal lining cells without any bleeding. 2) **Insertive anal intercourse without condom.** Studies suggest that men who participate only in this activity are at less risk of being infected than their partners who are rectally receptive; however, the risk is still significant. It carries high risk of infection by other sexually transmitted diseases. 3) **Vaginal intercourse without condom.**

Other STDs

Besides AIDS, other important sexually transmitted diseases to know about include syphilis, gonorrhea, herpes, venereal warts, hepatitis, intestinal parasites, crabs and scabies.

Syphilis is caused by bacteria. The germs enter you at one spot, usually on or near your cock, ass or mouth. 10–90 days (usually 21) after infection a small, open, painless sore called a chancre might develop at this spot. The chancre may not seem important, and it will go away after a while. Then, from two weeks to six months after infection, other vague signs might appear, such as a rash of small bumps over all or part of the body (including the palms and soles), patches of hair falling out, mild fever, or swollen lymph nodes. These signs will also go away within 2–6 weeks. Then it seems like the disease is gone, but actually it settles inside and over a period of years may cause serious damage to the heart, brain or other organs.

After the germs enter your body, they spread throughout the bloodstream. Another person can catch the germs through sexual contact, or by touching the chancre or rash when they develop. You're infectious to others as long as you have the disease.

If any of these signs or a friend warns you that you may have gotten syphilis, the only sure way to tell is through a blood test (and this test, by the way, can only show results after four weeks of infection, as the germs take that long to spread through the body). It's a good idea to have regular blood tests (every 3–6 months if you're sexually active) to make sure. Syphilis is easily cured with appropriate drugs, but any serious internal damage that's happened to the body can't be reversed. And as with all STDs, a syphilis infection stresses the body's immune system defenses.

Gonorrhea is caused by bacteria which infect a particular part of the body, cock, asshole or mouth. The germs can be passed from the infected area of one person to an uninfected part of another during sex. It can go from ass to cock, cock to ass and cock to mouth. Cock to cock isn't very likely. The disease is easily cured by antibiotics. If it's left untreated, however, it eventually causes serious sickness.

The signs of gonorrhea in the cock are a burning sensation when you pee and a milky discharge (drip, pus) from the tip. These symptoms will usually develop 2–10 days after sex with an infected person, though they may not appear at all. If your ass becomes infected, there'll probably be no sign of it at all (though sometimes there's a discharge, some blood or uncomfortable sensations). In the throat you might have some soreness, although this is also unlikely.

The only sure way to tell if you have gonorrhea is through a lab culture done on the suspected area. If you're suspicious get it checked out, and if you have intercourse with somebody you're not sure of, it's best to have a culture done every 3–6 months to make sure.

Also, be aware that several other infections can make your cock drip. These are known collectively as *non-gonococcal urethritis* (NGU), and are easily treated with antibiotics.

Herpes is caused by a virus that infects a particular area of the body, usually the lips, mouth, cock, asshole, up inside the rectum, or the groin or butt area. The incubation period is 2–20 days, and symptoms may start with a minor rash or itching at the infected spot, which then develops into painful blister-like, fluid-filled sores, often accompanied by swollen lymph nodes, fever, aching muscles and fatigue. The sores usually dry up and disappear within a week to a month, and the other symptoms clear up as well. But the virus settles in nearby nerves and may cause new outbreaks of sores when triggered by physical or emotional stress.

The virus is spread only during the open sore stage, through direct contact with the sores. In this way it can be spread through cock sucking, ass fucking, rimming, kissing and JO. A condom may not give protection when sores are active. It's safe to have sex when the sores have completely healed.

There's no cure for herpes. Treatment may be given for pain and to help prevent bacterial infection of the sores. You should keep the affected area clean and dry if possible.

Venereal warts are caused by the papilloma virus, which is spread through direct sexual contact with the infected area. Warts can infect the asshole, up inside the rectum, or on or near the penis. Near the ass they may be pink and moist with a broccoli-like shape, and on or near the cock they may be yellow-gray and hard to the touch. The incubation period is 1–3 months.

The warts are treated with a special liquid to destroy them, or they can be burned or frozen off or surgically cut when they're far up the rectum. If not treated, warts can keep spreading. Even with treatment they can grow back, so you should be examined again after several weeks to make sure, and re-treated if necessary. Besides causing ugly bumps, the wart virus may be implicated in the development of certain rectal cancers, so it's a good idea not to catch or spread them around.

Hepatitis is caused by several viruses that attack the liver. The incubation period can range from 15 days to as long as six months. A common early symptom is malaise, variously described as tiredness, easy susceptibility to fatigue, or lack of energy. Other symptoms are flu-like, including mild fever, joint aches, loss of appetite, nausea, vague stomach pains, weight loss, and sometimes diarrhea. About one or two weeks later new symptoms may develop, such as dark-colored pee, light-colored shit, a yellow cast to the skin and eyewhites, or itchy skin.

There's no cure for hepatitis. The disease is managed by proper rest, diet and care. Usually the major symptoms will disappear within a few weeks, but some malaise may persist for months afterward. It's also possible to get a hepatitis infection with very mild or no symptoms at all. More than a million people a year get hepatitis in the U.S. and more than four thousand die from it, a great many of them gay men.

The hepatitis virus can be spread through infected shit, during rimming for example, through infected come, when swallowing it or getting it injected up your rectum, and through infected saliva during deep, prolonged wet kissing. Also be aware that some people after getting hepatitis become chronic long-term carriers who can continue infecting others with it.

There's a vaccine you can take to prevent hepatitis B (one of the three kinds: A and *non-A*, *non-B* are the others); B is the kind most often spread among gay men during sex. Even though inoculation can be expensive, I encourage you to check it out with a doctor or a gay or county health clinic. Also, if you've been exposed to the disease, a shot of gamma globulin (for A) or immune globulin (for B) may prevent sickness if taken soon after infection.

To protect yourself from exposure to the hepatitis virus, it's a good idea to cut out rimming and to keep clean during and after sex. Wearing a condom during fucking might help prevent getting it that way. If you think you may have been exposed, it's important to see a doctor. If hepatitis is diagnosed, it's also important to tell anyone you may have exposed. Additionally, be aware that getting hepatitis can put the immune system under a great deal of stress.

There are several other vital infections that can be transmitted through come and other body fluids, and that have generally flu-like symptoms. These include *cytomegalovirus* infection and *infectious mononucleosis*, caused by the Epstein-Barr virus. As with hepatitis, blood tests can determine if you have an infection and what kind it is. All viral diseases have no cure, but are treated with rest and care.

Intestinal diseases infect the digestive tract. Symptoms can be nonexistent to severe, and include diarrhea, which may come and go, cramping, nausea, vomiting, fever and weakness. Symptomless people can still be carriers.

These diseases are spread through shit, so you could get them by rim-

ming or fucking somebody infected, through dirty fingers, contaminated lubricant, shared anal sex toys and so on.

The main intestinal diseases are *amebiasis*, caused by a one-celled parasite; *shigellosis*, caused by a bacterium; and *giardiasis*, caused by another parasite. Diagnosis is made by examining the person's shit, and may take several tries to confirm. The treatment medicines can sometimes cause unpleasant side effects, but it's important to clear up any of these infections completely. All the intestinal diseases can be very stressful to the body.

Crabs and *scabies* are two kinds of minute insect parasites that live on or under the skin. They're easily spread when rubbing bodies together, or from clothes and towels used by someone who has them. They both cause persistent itching. Crabs look a little like tiny versions of the shell-fish and love to crawl around in warm hairy spots, depositing tiny oval egg cases on hairshafts; the egg cases are one way to recognize when they're around. Scabies often look like flea bites, but the tiny insects are burrowing just under the skin; it's the body's reaction to their presence that produces the spots and itching. After infection with crabs, it takes a few days to a couple weeks before you might start to notice unusual itch-iness, and with scabies it can take 3–5 weeks. Neither of these infections is serious, and the insects are killed by coating your body with a treat-ment liquid and washing all your clothes and bedding. Also, try to warn anyone who may have been infected.

3

MASTURBATION

Masturbate, and then
you can wed the wind!

A satyr masturbating. Ancient Greek amphora. Museums of Berlin.

Self-portrait of photographer Franco of San Francisco's Ram Studios.

MASTURBATION

This chapter is about ways of sexual pleasuring with yourself and with others, that use the hands and penis. This is masturbation (jacking off), always popular, and surprisingly varied in the world of nature and humanity.

Captive apes and monkeys, as well as other animals, have been seen fondling their penis with hand or foot (or even taken into the mouth). In one study, young male chimpanzees were noticed handling each other's penis. Other limbs can be used too, such as with free-living spider monkeys and baboons, who use their tails. And elephants sometimes employ their trunks.

A curious scientist watches a porcupine:

> His excitement was evidenced by . . . holding a long stick in his fore paws and straddling it as a child does a broom-stick. The stick was held so that his genitals were stimulated by the contact, and the wood soon accumulated odor from the urine and glandular secretions absorbed. In consequence, it was a natural source of sexual stimulation.

Dolphins can be seen rubbing their erect penis against the tank floor, and one individual had the habit of holding his in the jet of the water intake. In addition, larger males will attempt masturbation against the flanks of smaller ones. Perhaps the most unusual way of masturbating is found among red deer:

> This act is accomplished by lowering the head and gently drawing the tips (of the antlers) to and fro through the herbage. Erection and extrusion of the penis from the sheath follows in five to seven seconds. . . . Ejaculation follows about five seconds after. . . .

History

Masturbation has always been common among humans. In some ancient western cultures, it was connected with religious worship. For example, in Egyptian mythology the god Orisis "creates all living creatures by an infinite act of masturbation." This was also seen as the source of the Nile river, and the cause of its annual flooding, which was the backbone of life in Egypt. The ritual developed of pharaohs masturbating before the god's image at the time of their enthronement. This led to public masturbation during religious worship, "to expel evil and honor the gods of generation," and became a part of ancient Egyptian, and also Phoenician, Babylonian and Assyrian, sacred ceremonies. Masturbation was also done for its own sake, without any sacred meanings; the Bible gives us several instances of this (the "spilling of seed").

The Greeks and Romans thought masturbation was invented by the god Hermes (Mercury in Latin). The Greeks called it *thrypsis*, "the rubbing" and in Latin it was *masturbatus*. People doubtless masturbated together at times, as well as doing it by themselves, in these ancient cultures, even though we have no records of this. The Ancients were generally very relaxed about male sexual expression. However, jacking-off was later frowned upon thoroughly by the Christian Church.

In the middle and far east, attitudes toward jacking-off have not changed from ancient times. In most eastern cultures, Arabian, Indian, Chinese, and Japanese, masturbation was allowed at an early age, and at times even encouraged. For example, Ibn Kemal Pasha, in *On the Lengthening and Thickening of the Rod* quotes old Arabian doctors in saying that "rubbing and constant handling doth make the virile member longer and thicker." Masturbation was sometimes used on babies to quiet their crying, and Bernard Stern noted that in Arabia it (jacking-off) "has become almost the custom of the land." Two scholars noted that Muslim and Jewish boys who actively and exclusively engaged in solitary and/or mutual masturbation, did so on the average of three to five times per week during the ages of eleven and eighteen.

In Arabian slang the act was known as *jeng, jelq, jerk*, and *musht-zeni*, jerking, flipping, jiggling and fist-beating respectively, referring to the different techniques. In Turkey it was called *istimney-bilyet* ("the practice of self-control of the stalk"), while in Persia it was called *maulish-e-zubb* ("shampooing the cord"). Masturbation was especially popular in public baths, where you and/or a friend, or a masseur and/or a prostitute, could engage you in the practice, "mutual or one-sided, as desired." Some ribald

poetry survives, such as two lines from "The Fabulous Feats of the Fut-
tering Freebooters:" "Felah the Negro did jerk off his yard/For all of a
week; hashish kept it up hard." And from the Persian poet Abu Nuwas:

Are not this child's eyes all fire?
    O desire,
Feel the first flush of the eggs
    Between his legs!
Dearest, seize what you can seize,
    If you please;
Fill your boyish fist with me
    And then see
Will it go a little way,
    Just in play?

In India, masturbation has a long history, going back to ancient Hindu
mythology. In one story, Lord Shiva was "masturbated by Agnee the Fire-
lord who, bearing his precious semen across the Ganges, accidentally
dropped it and witnessed the miraculous birth of Kartikeh (or Koomareh)
the misogynist war-god." Krishna, as god of Self-contemplation, became
the symbol of jacking-off and "the favorite Hindoo youth. His practice,
hautrus (manual orgasm) . . . was deified as ritualistic." It was also called
panimathana ("hand churning") and "was relished extensively."

In China, Dr. Jacobus reports, young men would get together to
smoke opium, and then "abuse their generative organs for hours at a time
in a a frenzy of mutual masturbation and anal copulation." Along the same
lines, one report explains that the Cossacks, who lived on the middle Asian
plains, were more excited by self and mutual masturbation than in sex with
women, "having from infancy identified sexual pleasure with masturbation alone."

Among other cultures, masturbation was often allowed or encouraged.
Of special interest are cultures allowing the act to be shared between males.
These include the Hopi in Arizona, Wogeo in Oceania, and Dahomeans
and Namu of Africa. In certain Melanesian communities this was expected
between boys, and between boys and married men, although no other kind
of gay male sex was allowed. In the Cubeo tribe of the Amazon, mutual
masturbation was "semi-public." Among the Tikopia of the south Pacific,
men masturbated themselves as other men watched.

Techniques—by Yourself

Masturbation is a joy. I am thoroughly convinced that God gave people hands with fingers so that we could stroke ourselves in pleasure and comfort. Those men who've not discovered the satisfaction of jacking off, are definitely missing something.

There is only one problem I can think of in masturbating, that someone would think it was a bad thing to do, would feel guilty during and after, or worse yet wouldn't do it altogether. The suppression of pleasurable masturbation is one of the great ills of our society, for masturbation is one of the basic functions of existence; those who deny or ignore it do so at the risk of increasing their own sense of frustration and grimness in the world.

Jacking off, besides feeling good, serves many useful purposes. It can be relaxing, reassuring, energizing, encouraging, spontaneous and charming. You can do it quick, slow, with hands, pillows, melons and showers, in a bathroom, behind a bush or on the bus, dry or with oils, while listening to music, looking at pictures, or imagining. It is an anywhere, anytime convenience. And don't be afraid to indulge. When your body's had enough, it'll say so.

One main trouble in masturbating is to not be embarrassed. You could get caught! The best ways to overcome this inconvenience are to make sure you'll have privacy, learn to do it quick, and/or learn to do it in public without being found out. All of these are quite possible.

I remember once I was at a picnic, and I was standing in a crowd. It was so hot that many people had taken off their shoes and shirts. Then I saw across from me such a beautiful boy that I almost had to leave, I got so excited. Luckily, I was wearing my old baggy navy pants, and the pockets were worn through. I slung my coat over my right shoulder to hide my arm, and plunged my hand down my pocket, walking into the crowd as close as I could get. I had a great time, and I'm sure that not one of the hundreds of people around me guessed a thing about it! (Note: for tricks of this sort, wear tight-fitting underpants to catch the come, or learn to hold your ejaculation inside when you come, so you don't make a sticky mess.)

Mechanically speaking, masturbation for males is friction against the *fraenum*, or "whang-string," a small, string-like portion of the penis just under the glans or "head" at the backside. The fraenum has the highest concentration of sexsensual nerve endings in the body. Many actions can stimulate this area; an object can rub against the penis, the penis can move against something, or no motion can happen at all. This last might easily happen, since fantasy and mind stimulation play such a big role; wet

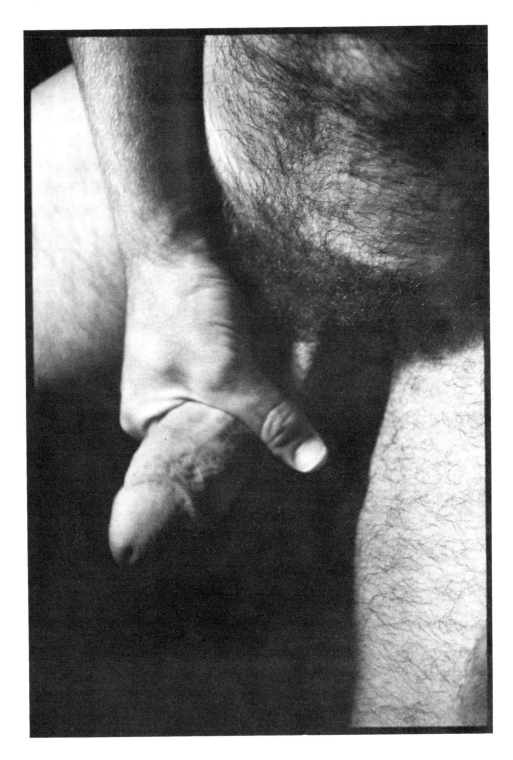

dreams are a good example of this. I have a friend who sometimes comes to orgasm while meditating, after his yoga practice.

Although I'll restrict myself here to "jacking-off," using the hand, be aware that with a little imagination and creativity other ways can be found. There are many things you can discover about yourself with your hands. The hands are very sensitive to touch, and the penis is even more so.

Every person develops their own way of jacking off. If you've ever had others do it to you, you discover that usually they can't make the feelings quite as good as you can yourself. That's because you're probably using their style on you, which fits for them but isn't yours. Style involves such things as how the fingers hold the penis, which fingers are used, how tight they are, how hard they press, how much movement, use of the foreskin, and how much sensitivity towards drawing out the feelings. All these are important.

Some people like to wrap the whole hand around their penis and slide it all the way up and down in long, luxurious strokes, using oils or a flexible foreskin. Others like to place thumb and two fingers around the corona (that part of the penis just below the glans), with one finger over the fraenum, and pump in short, quick movements with the skin.

There is room for exploration and creativity in masturbation. Fantasy plays a big part, and in your mind you can be loving someone else or yourself. You can imagine your last sexual act, or an erotic fantasy, or looking at pictures or a story. Fantasies are especially intriguing; they are the images and events of your inner and secret wishes. Even if they seem strange or something you wouldn't want anyone to find out about—that's OK—who's going to know if you don't tell?

Loving yourself through masturbation means caressing your own body, holding it, making love to you, appreciating you/your experience as hand and penis, body and mind. It's unique.

A Masturbation Fantasy

Let me take you on a fantasy: you'll need privacy and quiet, some enjoyable music (something warm and not too loud), candles and oil (olive oil, safflower oil, massage or love oil, baby/mineral oil, vaseline, KY or any clean lubricating substance are all good). It's night time outside. First, light the candles, put on the music, and turn off the lights. Then remove your clothes and, lying down on the bed, close your eyes. Take a deep, relaxing breath. Imagine that you are a stranger meeting your body, that it's new to you, that you're touching it for the first time. Start at the top of your head,

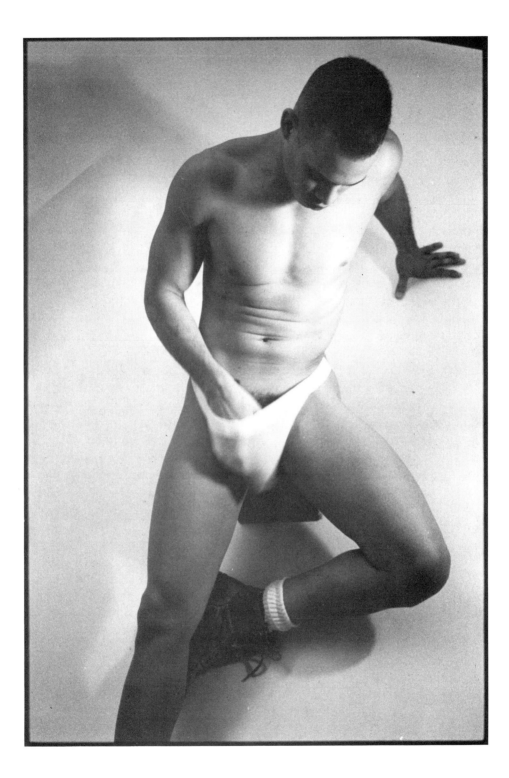

and explore yourself with your hands, as sensations you've never felt before. Feel your hair, the shape of your head, then your face, your ears. Glide your fingers over each part, trying to feel the shape, the texture, as if you'd never felt them before. Notice the softness of your eyelids, the sensitivity of your lips. Then caress your throat, your shoulders and chest. Find a nipple, and flick a fingertip over and around it, feeling it grow hard and excited. Glide your palms over your stomach, pressing down on your soft middle. Trace designs around your navel. Slowly let your hands press lower. Discover how your pubic hair begins; how does it feel? Seek out the lines where your legs join your stomach. Trace the line with your fingertip down into the groove between leg and crotch, until you brush your testicles. Press your soft, warm hands onto the insides of your thighs. Stroke your thighs, feeling their sensitivity, their shape, their thickness. Brush the hair lightly. Then discover how your ass ends underneath. Then glide up under your testicles, tracing a ring around them. Hold them warmly in your hand, feeling each, then press them gently against your body. Now discover the shape of your penis with one fingertip. Trace a line around the base, then up the side to the top. Lightly brush the side, the fraenum, the glans and tip. Wrap one hand carefully around the whole penis, and squeeze gently. Pull on it a little, then let it go. Find the fraenum with your fingertip, and press there (You may have to pull down your foreskin). Discover the most sensitive point, and brush your fingertip rapidly just over that point. Press your finger there again and massage the point gently and firmly. Then wrap your hand around your penis and move it up and down.

Now put some oil in the cup of your hand, and caress your penis all over, rubbing and massaging the oil evenly. Cradle your testicles in one hand, and wrap the other around your penis. Slide your hand up and down all the way, feeling the sensations. Explore until you develop a pleasing rhythm, and sink into the warmth and pleasure. Go deeper and warmer, letting the feelings grow stronger and spread. If you want to increase sensation or stretch your foreskin, hold down the base of your penis with thumb and forefinger of the other hand, pulling the skin tight. Keep stroking yourself, pausing if you like to explore somewhere else. Your sensations will become stronger in a growing cycle of tension and relaxation. Discover your pattern and try to draw it out. Explore the way(s) to climax, fast or slow, with long or short strokes, pumping fast and rough, or gentle and calming until your heat rises pouring out of you. Let yourself go, flow into it. Then relax. Relax deeply, doing nothing, emptying your mind and body. Peacefulness.

This fantasy can be done just as well in the tub or shower, using soap instead of oil. An interesting variation is to do it in front of a mirror. You can

52

watch yourself, your hands and body, in new ways.

An exciting addition to masturbation can be using a finger to caress your ass (called *postillioning*). While masturbating, simply grease a finger (don't use soap) and press it at your anus-opening, pushing firmly and gently to slide inside. You'll have to discover how best to place your body so that reaching is easy; I suggest bending your knees and bringing your feet to your rear, while lying on your back, or even stretching your feet over your head. You can also do this standing up.

Masturbation is an act of wholeness, of self creation and renewal, whether it's a five-minute quickie or a half-hour journey. You can become more you, more together and centered through deep and satisfying masturbation. The moment of climax is a moment of infinity, and under your control. Also, be aware of the limitations of masturbation, the things it can't get you, like another persons' touching and love. Admitting your needs is the first step to satisfying them.

Surprisingly enough, masturbation, body image, and other kinds of sex are all related. If you like and enjoy your body, it will show in your masturbation. Poor opinion of your body is a good thing to recognize and deal with. Just be aware; tune in on yourself; let yourself be and then do

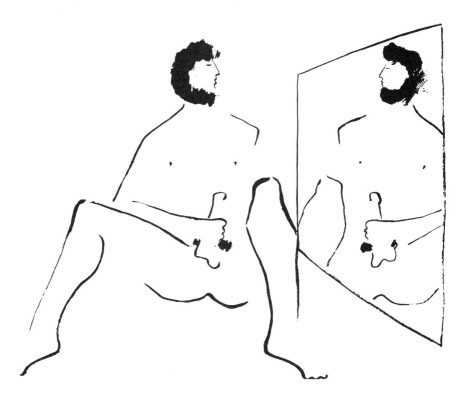

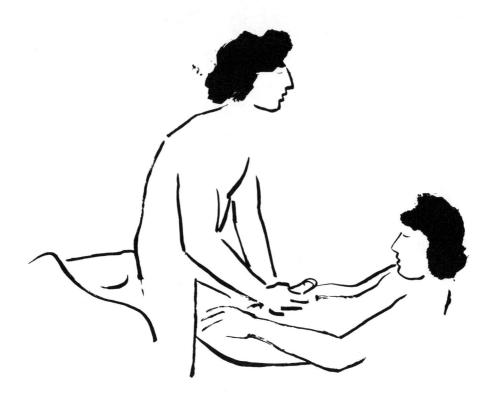

what needs to be done. Once you sense a problem here, it's good to talk it over with a friend or counselor.

A sense of relaxation and intimacy with your body is akin to being intimate with another, and he with you. If you don't want to be sensual with your own crotch, how can you keep this from carrying over? Be aware of yourself as the source of *all* your experiences, ideas and feelings.

Also, masturbation is a favorite shared experience. Whether you're jacking yourself off while he watches, or you him, or using masturbation during fellatio (sucking) or anal intercourse (fucking), it's a basic experience and action. Throughout this book, masturbation will be mentioned again and again as a pleasurable activity with other actions or by itself. It serves as a good foundation for any kind of sexual and/or intimate sharing, with others and with yourself.

It's good to respect jacking-off and be relaxed about it. Many people find it their favorite sexual activity, either alone or with others, but don't want to admit the fact for being thought unsophisticated or immature.

That's nonsense—no one is immature for liking to jack off, or to prefer it over fucking. Masturbation is entirely pleasurable and wholesome. Only boredom, unhappiness, hard work and so on are dull things in bed. If you like to jack off by yourself enjoy it. If you like to masturbate with your friend(s), good for you. Make sure you let him know this, and take into account his desires too.

I remember once when I was with someone I thought "sophisticated," and I thought I should be sucking and fucking, because it was the "sophisticated" thing to do. But surprise of surprises when he blurted out to me he really wanted to masturbate himself while I cuddled his balls; he was even embarrassed about it! So I gave him a big hug, and we wound up having a fine time together. He was a beautiful man.

Techniques—with Another

One of the most intimate and joyful experiences to share is mutual masturbation. Lying with a friend, allowing yourself to be caressed and stroked, he trusting you, openly, your hand holding his testicles—you both doing it together, or he lying back luxuriously, in your hands, or you masturbating yourself with his hand on your thigh—there's a lot of meaning and experience here!

This is more than just a way to release sexual tension; it's *being* and *sharing*, and maybe growing as well. All these are open for you to explore, if you feel calm with him, safe about yourself and your desires.

If you feel rushed, slow down and see what happens. It is possible to really savor the feel of his penis in your hand, its touch and thickness, firmness and warmth. Remember the masturbation fantasy in the first section? Well, it's just as much fun to give it to someone else, as to do it yourself. And you may learn quite a bit, by seeing how another is similar and different to you. In the shape and feel of his body, in the way he's aroused and climaxes, in his sexual style.

Earlier on I spoke of people developing their individual way of masturbating. You'll be surprised how much variety there is. Talk with him, and find out how he likes your hand, if he'd rather you held him differently, and so on. There's much to share, if you want to open up.

Mutual masturbation can be close and wet, hot and fast, or it can be much different, slow and relaxed for example. It's all a matter of opening up to how you are at that moment, what you want and need. Maybe you're scared, and just want to be held. Or perhaps you're tired and would like him to jack you off casually. Or maybe you really want to abandon yourself in love-making.

If you are uptight about masturbating, jacking-off while he watches can be great therapy. Many of us tend to feel guilty about masturbation, from having to hide it when we were younger. With him, you can be open, and lose your fear to the light. And many of us are also guilty about receiving pleasure—we feel we always have to reciprocate, to give it back immediately. Try just lying back sometimes and not doing a thing, and let him do everything; just relax, just receive.

There are lots of other things you can do with masturbation. You can massage his body all over. Each of you can masturbate himself while you hold the other's testicles—some friends told me they had highly spiritual/loving experiences during this. Also it can be a lot of fun not taking your clothes off, as if you'd just met and grabbed each other on the street, or with your underpants still on (jockey shorts really turn me on). Another treat can be taking a shower together, standing under the spigot masturbating each other with plenty of soap. If you both like, you can massage his ass at the same time. Since body tension can affect intensity of climax, you can try different positions while being masturbated: sitting up, crouching over him, or hanging from the ceiling for example. You can fondle each other without climaxing, or without even getting hard. This can be specially delightful and warm, as the caring/trust/sharing comes more to the fore. You can even have a lot of fun in public, seeing if you can fondle each other on the bus or in a restaurant without anyone knowing.

There's almost always a free hand available, and it doesn't take much energy. At times your arm might get a little tired; if this happens, relax for a while. Masturbating someone else is different than with yourself, because you aren't directly experiencing: you must rely on him to let you know how it's going, and this may not be clear. With yourself, it's simple to know when to speed up and when to slow down or stop.

Discovering how to do this with someone else can be a fun exploration. Ask him how he's doing. I've had times where the person wasn't holding me right—his thumb wasn't quite in the right place, and when I came it wasn't quite as good. It's OK not to be the perfect sex partner, or have the perfect time. But don't be afraid to complain, too. If you're jerking him off, stop when you like, except if he's just before climax (coming). If you stop too close to ejaculation, the process will continue anyway but the experience might be second-rate. Other than this, I'd be pretty loose about it and see what happens. Try experimenting with different strokes and hand grips, with and without oil. Cradling his balls in the other hand and kissing him, all at the same time, can be especially nice.

Learning to communicate sensations, wants, and needs is always an important part of being with someone. It comes with experience and relaxation. Remember that he can't read your mind, be directly aware of your experiences, nor you with him. There is the space between you to cross over. How you do it is up to you: words, questions, grunts, moaning; don't just assume he knows what's going on, or that you should know how he's doing without his telling you—some people are rather quiet and might not say anything. When in doubt, you can always ask, and better to ask than be fearful of relaxing your arm for a moment.

Some question may come up about simultaneous orgasms, coming at the same time. "Should we or shouldn't we?" My opinion is, it's nice if it happens and nice if it doesn't. It's not always easy to know when someone's going to climax, and it can be harder still to coordinate two climaxes. Why let work take away from pleasure? It's good to experiment with this and see what's most satisfactory; for some couples it's easier than for others. The best thing is usually to be loose about it, preferring spontaneity over planning, and feeling over thinking. But by all means, if you indulge in pleasure it's hard not to have a good time.

Related Happenings

I would like to mention some related ways to get off. These are body rubbing, interfemoral intercourse, armpit/knee intercourse, and moving on the perineum.

Body rubbing (also known as the "Princeton rub") is a common activity, and some people find it their favorite. It's a kind of masturbation with another, except no hands are used. You are lying together, moving with and on each other, usually side by side or above/below. This is usually done "dry," that is without lubrication, but oiling large parts of your bodies and then slipping 'n sliding can also be lots of fun (and messy). Not everyone likes this kind of sex; some people find their penis just gets chafed and numb from body hair and skin. If you get into it, one or both of you can move at a time, up and down, wriggling around and/or *thrusting* with the pelvis (tipping the pelvis up and back to move the penis).

A related activity is called interfemoral intercourse, "the Oxford style." Here one of you lies on your back, with your thighs held tight together. Then your friend lies on top of you, and either dry or greasing his penis and the insides of your thighs, inserts his penis between your legs just below your crotch. He then thrusts his penis in and out. To some people this may seem like a strange activity, but to others (and in some cultures) it's quite common.

Interfemoral intercourse can also be done from behind, with one of you lying on your stomach. This leads us to another related method, which is thrusting between your friend's buttocks, without entering his anus. A lubricant can also be used here. Again, some people enjoy this way, and it has had its place in other cultures (the ancient Greeks, for example, called it *pygisma*, "buttockry").

Armpit/Knee Intercourse: If you make a tight, firm place by holding your arm at your side or your knee bent, he can insert his penis (lubricated if necessary) at the joint and slide in and out by moving his body. He can even climax this way.

Another way is moving on the perineum, the space between the testicles and anus, where the legs meet. This is a very tender area, and when lubricated feels nice to the penis. One of you lies on your back, bringing your knees to your chest. The other, then, lies down between his friend's legs facing him, with his penis resting at the perineum. Body motions and thrusting will create pleasurable sensations, and kissing is quite easy.

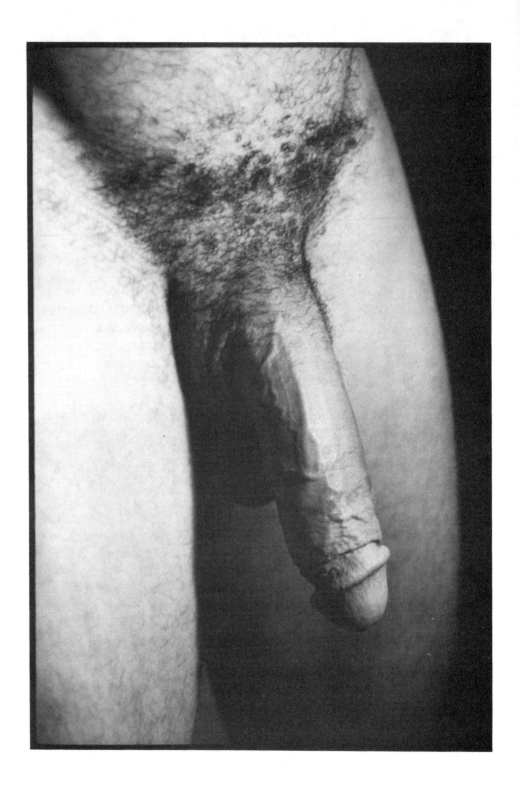

4

FELLATIO

O Thaïs, no one is too old to get sucked off.

—Martial

The Muslims call them "banana eaters."

—Dr. Jacobus

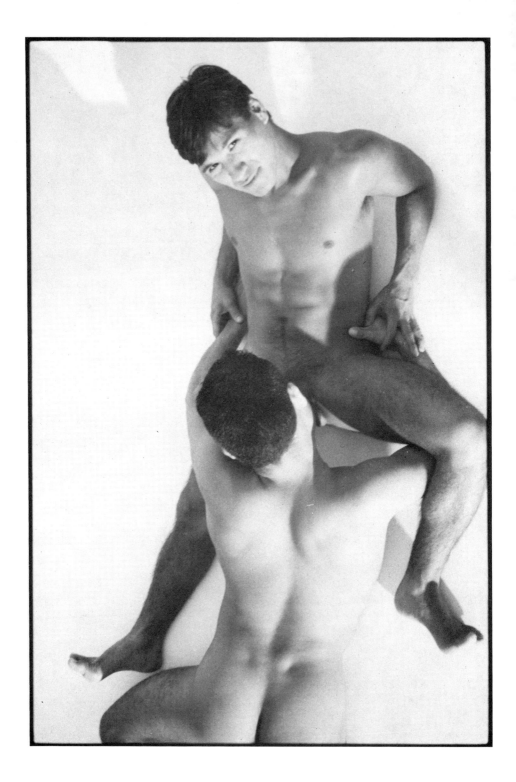

FELLATIO

This chapter is devoted to pleasurable union of the mouth and penis, also known as oragenitalism, inosculation, fellation, irrumation, a blow job, to head, suck (off), eat, blow, suck cock, lick dick, blowing the meat whistle, playing the skin-flute, cop-a-jock, kneeling at the altar, tooting the flute, and scalper le mochican, among many others. For simplicity's sake I'll use the term fellatio (from the Latin "to suck"), or just "sucking."

History

The delights of fellatio were probably savored even in the dawn of civilization. Maybe the early Middle Easterners learned it "in the most natural manner: by observing nature," that is, by watching domesticated and wild animals licking each other's genitals—"thus, from natural observation, investigation, and experimentation, emerge the arts of love." As the Old Testament so often reminds us, the Jews were surrounded by incorrigible sodomites, the Babylonians, Philistines, Chaldeans, Egyptians, etc. who, we can be sure, didn't ignore penis-sucking when it came time to have a good time. There are very old Egyptian pictures that seem to suggest fellatory activity.

In ancient Greece, fellatio was known as "playing the flute." Its praises were sung by Greek and Roman poets, and so it must have been fairly widespread. Priapus comments, "Through the middle of boys and girls travels the member; when it meets bearded chins then it aspires to the heights." The Roman poet Martial counsels an aging friend, "Why do you plague in vain unhappy vulvas and posteriors; gain but the heights, for there any old member revives." And the poet Lucian mentions the fellatory rape of the Syrian Timarchus:

In Egypt, on the other hand, they called you "sore throat"—and this is a well-known business. It must have been a close thing with you not to be choked, that time you came across the sailor of a three-master, who fell upon you and stopped up your throat for you!

Lucian even tells us that Timarchus enjoyed the "active" as well as "passive" roles.

In the Medieval period fellatio is lumped together with anal intercourse under the accusatory label "sodomia," so documents relating to its use and popularity become uncertain. However, based on general estimates of homosexual activity, fellatio doubtless continued to be practiced throughout Europe until modern times.

We can't be certain of the frequency among gay male acts, of fellatio in a population. Magnus Hirschfeld's pioneering research around the turn of this century in Germany estimates that 40% of gay males practice one-way and mutual fellatio. In most cultures anal intercourse is the most common form of gay male sexual activity. An exception to this is found

Scene from an orgy. Attributed to Skythes.
An Attic cup. The Louvre, Paris

Twentieth Century study. Woodcut. Artist unknown

among the Crow Indians of North America. Among them, anal intercourse is absent and fellatio "fairly frequent."

In India the art of fellatio has a long history, going back perhaps "to the birth of Christ." One of the first love manuals, the *Kama Sutra* (ca. 100–300 A.D.) has a whole chapter on *oparishtaka*, "mouth congress," saying that

> The male servants of some men carry on the mouth congress with their masters. It is also practised by some citizens, who know each other well, among themselves.

In India it is also known as *mukhamethuna* ("oral churning") and *ambarchusi* ("mango-fruit sucking").

Fellatio has been highly praised from North Africa eastward, being "common and customary among all classes and races," often

> deemed even more intimate and enrapturing than genital union, perhaps because oral excitation yields the most acute and intense pleasure. The sensations produced by the caressing mouth of one's beloved seem more ardent and enravishing than those produced by the penis or vagina.

In Turkey, it's felt that

fellatio allows greater variety and subtler nuances of pleasure than vaginal or anal activity, which are more or less restricted in their execution and effect. In a word, as the Turks say, "Penis sucking is better than fucking!"

Throughout the Arab world, the slang word for fellatio is *qerdz*. In Tunisia, Egypt, Arabia, Persia, Afghanistan, and farther, to Malaya, from which there is this sex-party account:

The scene is the same all over the room. While the man lies at full length on a couch or sits reclined in a chair, the boy—kneeling or stooping—holds and kisses his penis, sucks it, and receives the emission of semen in his mouth, right up to the very last drop.

In all, there are many places in the world where the finer joys were and are savored and cultivated. The "Arabian voluptuary" as Victorian England knew him, or the "damnable Toork" of an earlier era, could appreciate a darting tongue, wet, firm lips, and sucked-in cheeks clinging to a quivering stalk.

Basic Techniques

There's no proper or best way to do fellatio. There's only two people, each unique, wanting to share some interest. And each has their own wants and needs to satisfy. These can't be fit into the "correct" way, a certain pattern good for all, at all times. You must find your own way, what's good and comfortable for you.

Sucking, like rubbing and fucking, is another way for two people to share pleasure, touch, and care. Specific skills, techniques, and positions are not as important as your consciousness about fellatio and the other person and yourself, at that moment in time. You'll do fine, if your frame of mind is in harmony with yourself and your surroundings. In Harmony: easy, relaxed, feeling safe, OK. You are a changing, alive being, and your mood will suit different activities at different times.

Sex is fun—that's why I do it. It gives me satisfaction for my friend to

suck my cock, and for me to suck his. Let this be your inner guide, and you will do good by yourself and your friend. Notice, I'm not saying "you should have fun doing fellatio." I'm saying fellatio *is* joyful: sunny, agreeable, charming, cozy, giving, luxurious, passionate, inviting—if you're not having any of these, you're not doing fellatio, you're doing something else. When it stops being fun, it's time to stop, and find out what happened.

Fellatio is easy to do—all it is, is a penis and mouth touching; a kiss in passing is fellatio. *How* they touch can involve anything you want to do, for as long as you want to do it. The most common form of fellatio has one person lying relaxed, on his back, and his friend fellates him.

It might seem like one person is getting all the pleasure as the other gives it—this is not true; each gives to the other and to himself: one gives his penis, the other his mouth; one gives his trust, the other his care; one feels the warm, caressing mouth, the other feels the strong, warm penis— and all are pleasing. It's true that the fellator doesn't always know what to do at first; he might be confused by old habits, cultural fears, or just inexperience—prolonged fellatio, like all human sex acts, must be learned, and learning anything takes time and patience.

Let's say you're with your friend, and you're kissing his body. Then you kiss his erect penis. This is a good chance to explore his penis with your mouth. How does it feel to your lips? Your tongue? Explore all around— feel its shape, its thickness, its soft skin; the textured crown on top, with its meatus or opening; the fraenum or string-like portion coming down from the head to the ring of skin called the corona; the foreskin if he has one; the scrotum (his balls) at the base—explore all these with your lips and tongue tip.

Then, if you both want, explore the penis inside your mouth—let your lips slide over the head and down the shaft a little (watch the teeth!). How does it feel to your lips and tongue now? Move them around some. If you like, slide your mouth down farther. Notice the feeling of stretch in your jaws, and if the penis gets close to your throat, the beginning of your gagging reflex. Now slide the penis out of your mouth slowly, and see how that feels. Pause for a moment, to let it sink in. You might ask your friend what he experienced.

If I'm doing this, sucking someone, I usually begin to experience a warm closeness. In fact, I usually only like to suck someone when I really care a lot for him, and want to give myself as closely as I can. It's so intimate a mingling of two people: my mouth, gentle, expressive, strong, wet, warm, my speechpart, the entrance for my breath, my lips; his crotch, his most sensitive, guarded physical center, his inner thighs, lower belly, testicles, and his thick pulsating penis rooted in and up through him. How delightful to share these. And his trust, his giving me his body, our mixing security and being.

There are lots of things to do with your mouth on his penis, like licking it all over, sucking on it, flicking your tongue tip rapidly across the top. One of the simplest and nicest actions is to move your mouth up and down on his penis. This is called *sliding*. Make a ring with your lips around the shaft. You'll need a thick padding of saliva to avoid irritation and give the richest, warmest sensations—don't be afraid of it, it's in the spirit of mud pies when you were a kid, and just as fun.

You can slide slow or fast, and take as much penis into your mouth as you like. One neat action is to slide down as far as you can, and then draw his penis out slowly while sucking on it, like a peppermint stick.

For a more intense activity, you can slide faster and/or go deeper with your strokes. And for an even warmer closeness, you can also fondle and cup his balls in your hand, and add postillioning.

If you and he decide to bring him to orgasm, sliding is a nice way. If so, he'll probably appreciate stroking as fast and full as you can. Let me relate a few tips about this.

His experience will get more energetic and intense as he approaches orgasm. Your sliding will cause the most stimulation if you encircle your lips firmly around his penis and over the tips of your teeth. This makes a smooth, snug embrace, and helps avoid nips and amputations. Move your head up and down as if it were saying "yes," from just below the top of the penis to as far down as you like. Meanwhile, keep all the other parts of your mouth as relaxed as possible (actual "sucking" is not important

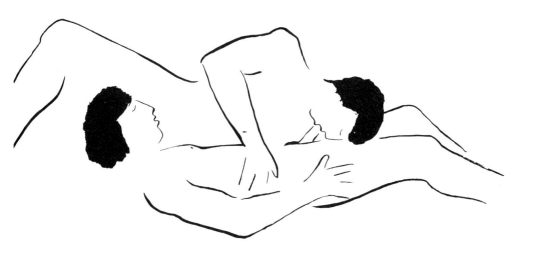

here). As you go faster and deeper, get into a regular rhythm. If things start to get very excited, you can move from your shoulders and upper back instead of your neck, so that you're bouncing up and down with your whole upper body. By using these muscles you give more energy to your strokes and avoid fatigue better.

If you're wary of gagging, you can wrap one hand around the bottom half of the penis and slide on the top part. If so, it's nice to move your hand up and down too, doing it so that as your lips move up to the fraenum, your hand moves down to strike against the base. This feels extra nice because it presses against the bone just above the penis (called the *mons pubis*) and also because your hand pulls the skin tight, which increases sensation. In fact, even if you don't use your hand too much, you can hold it at the base to pull the skin tight.

If you're really into giving every inch of goodness possible, you can add simultaneous sideways motions of your head. First, learn to do the sliding so it comes easily. Then, as you move up and down, rotate your head from side to side as if saying "no." The two motions need to be coordinated, so, for example, as you come up, turn your head from the center to the right, at the top turn your head to the left, and as you go down, back to the center.

Let me emphasize that the above actions take time to learn. The best way is by becoming familiar with one activity in an easy, relaxed way, and adding on from there. Doing a rapid slide may seem strange and uncomfortable, and if you experience it this way, it's best to take your time about learning it, and only when you feel *very safe*, that it's OK with your friend and you to slow down, stop, or whatever. Remember, none of these activities is any big deal. What counts is you having a good time.

Sometimes when I'm in my spiritual mood, I get into the feeling of this up-and-down motion on the erect penis. There's something very basic about it, as if I was sensing a bottomless glow coming up from below my mind. I believe that each of us has a genetic memory, a meaning as old and wise as the universe itself. We're not usually conscious of this, the base pattern for our life experiences. But the up-and-down on the penis is part of this pattern, and can trigger in us green-life warmth, as if the universe were saying, "Yes! This is very mysterious and good. Grow!" Pay attention and see what comes up.

Techniques to Explore

I'd like to list a few things you can explore during fellatio. Think of each as a possibility if it seems interesting at some time and place:

—*Around the World:* this is kissing and licking the body all over. As I mentioned before, this might end at the crotch, and lead right into fellatio. If you're moving down his stomach, you can kiss your way into his crotch, or use a somewhat pointy tongue in flicking motions within the groove of the crotch, between the thigh and testicles. You can tongue the scrotum itself, licking and cuddling his balls with a soft, caressing tongue, and even draw one or both into the mouth with very light sucking motions or humming (known as "chewing gum"). From here, you can massage the perineum, the space between the testicles and anus, and even go on to tongue the anus also, known as *rimming.*

—If you want to get the penis hard, or just to caress it soft, knead it with firm lips, or kiss and nibble at it all over, or suck hard on the crown.

—Also, if you make your tongue soft, thick, and rounded, you can cuddle the penis with broad, languorous lapping strokes, caressing and enveloping it. This is called *the Shirley Temple,* because it's like licking a big lollipop or sugar daddy.

—You can suck and tongue the top while masturbating the shaft with your hand, or by rolling the shaft between your two flattened palms, like rolling dough.

—If you want to try something very complex, while you're doing a rhythmical sliding with side to side motions, draw your tongue to the back of your mouth and as the penis is sliding in and out, circle and caress the glans and corona. You must have several free inches back there to get maneuverability, so don't try this when your mouth's stuffed full.

—There's also an Oriental style for doing the sliding action, where you move up and down from the waist, like an old washerwoman at the river, instead of from the neck. You must sit on his chest or between his legs to do this.

—If you can handle his penis in your throat, try putting it there and going through swallowing motions, or shaking your head around without otherwise moving it. These will give different sensations.

Body Positions

Let me describe a few positions, body arrangements, possible for two people during fellatio. There are two standard positions that are easy and satisfying. In both the person being fellated lies flat on his back. In the first, his partner lies on his side, facing head to feet. This allows for mutual fondling. In the second position, the partner sits or lies on his stomach between his friend's legs, facing him. This gives the fellator more movement and also puts his tongue against his friend's fraenum (this may or may not be important).

There are many other positions possible. Some allow mutual genital stimulation, or more body tension, or body contact. Here's a few:

—You're sitting, standing, or leaning against a wall or tree trunk. Your friend kneels in front of you to suck you off. This can be really fun in the shower.

—If you're on your back with your friend kneeling or sitting on your chest, you can easily reach up to fondle him and add rimming if you like.

—For an unusual experience, you can be lying upside down in a chair or car seat, so that your head is down and your knees bent over the back. Your friend, meanwhile, stands in the back seat and bends way over on his stomach between your legs.

In general, fellatio can be done with either one of you lying, on your side, sitting, or standing, in or out of doors. If you want to go exploring, there are lots of possibilities. Remember that you aren't restricted to the top of a bed. By using imagination and handy pieces of furniture, pillows, and rocks or trees if in the forest, you can get into some intriguing and unusual experiences. Be creative and mobile and see what happens.

Problems

Now I'd like to talk about a few problems that can happen while you're fellating someone. The first is gagging. This is a spontaneous, unwilled muscular defense of the throat when bumped against foreign objects. It's just a natural reaction, like jerking your hand away from fire. But often it's a source of embarrassment and confusion in one or both partners, during fellatio, ironically implying dislike or rejection. You can control gagging by not going too deep. Also, if you become very excited, the reflex is not likely to happen. If you're doing mutual fellatio (sixty-nine) you might have an exciting time and not even notice that his penis is going way back in your mouth.

Fortunately, the whole gagging reflex will decrease with experience. If you start out slow and calm, you'll see that it's not so scary. If you want, gently explore the sensations of his penis touching the inside and back of your mouth, over time. Experimenting with depth while doing the slide activity is a good way. Another way to help condition yourself is, while brushing your teeth, use the back of the toothbrush to explore around in your mouth. Be playful—try brushing your tongue, moving the brush a little farther back each time, to see how far down you can go.

Another possible problem is taking semen in your mouth. Cum is a curious thing. Its taste varies from person to person, mild to tangy. It's good stuff nutritionally, being mostly protein and minerals; it's the minerals that give the unique flavor. Keep in mind, however, that sucking to climax is considered an AIDS moderate-risk sex activity (see guidelines p. 37).

If you want to swallow it without hassle (when your partner is *definitely 100% HIV-negative*), take the climax deep in your mouth, and remember, "in each and every case, the faster it is swallowed, the less time the taste remains." Vomiting, noisy hawkings, or dashing to the bathroom can be very rude and demeaning to someone who's just climaxed, so if you don't want to swallow it, remove it quietly afterwards, into a handy towel or handerchief. Or if you like, switch from fellatio to masturbation or something else beforehand, but don't do this too close to orgasm.

A third possible problem is genital odor. All people have a natural smell. There's little connection between smell and venereal or other diseases; it's solely a matter of cleanliness. Some people enjoy a hearty smell, others can't tolerate even the slightest whiffs. Genital odor is one of the more intimate facts about a person, and can be the delight and turn-on to the warm closeness of fellatio. If not, it can often be ignored. Or you can escort him to the bathroom and wash him yourself.

A fourth possible problem is muscle fatigue. This is to be expected during fellatio—the mouth can get tired being stuffed full, and actions of the tongue and neck also take a lot of energy. It's a natural part of the sexplay pattern, and calls for a change of pace and/or position. It's probably not such a good idea just to stop and sit there panting or making nasty comments. If communication is easy between you and your partner, it will be understood and OK for each to do what you have to do, without being an irritant. Sometimes you might get tired just as he's getting ready to come, since this is a likely time for being energetic and lively. You can always slow down if it's not too close to orgasm, or switch to something easier. Also, this problem will happen less often as you become more used to fellatio, as you become more confident in yourself and your friend.

The last possible problem is a rising fear or even panic as he comes to orgasm. This can be caused by one or all of the problems I just mentioned, or just by the force and drive of impending orgasm, or by your current mood. Inexperience or distaste can be big contributors. You begin to feel like you've lost control, or something very bad is going to happen, and then the activity suffers, often at just the wrong moment.

There is a point at which the momentum towards climax is so strong that it will go ahead even if you slow down, and if you do stop just before, the orgasmic experience may be very second-rate. If you start to panic at

his orgasm, there's not much you can do about it but maintain as best you can. Afterwards you'd best deal with it unless you want it to happen again.

The important thing is to feel safe. Part of this is trusting yourself and your friend. Another part is to *know* what's coming. Often the first spurt of semen will trigger the gagging reflex, and cause a panic. Knowing that this might happen and that you can still continue sucking can keep you from freaking out. For a long time, I had a lot of trouble panicking before orgasm. Now I feel much better about it, through trust, experience, and by breaking down my problem into its parts (gagging, fatigue, etc.) and dealing with each. Talk about any problems with your partner and your friends. Just saying what you feel is often very helpful. Ask them if they experience these things and how they handle them.

Also remember that your current mood has a lot to do with your experience, and mood can shift a lot through time. One day you might feel quite happy to eat sperm, and the next think it's awful. It's important to respect your mood, and realize that it may change later.

And also, I'd like to say a word about letting go. In the kind of fellatio I've been talking about so far, one person is doing things with his friend's penis, while the other person just lies back and experiences. If your friend is sucking your penis, he, in a sense, has control which you, in a sense, have given to him (you always keep control over your own choices). This sense of not being in control can be frightening sometimes, the person feeling like he's losing himself, his power, security. He's not safe. If you start feeling this way, don't try to force yourself to be strong: this gives more strength to the fear. Instead, just be aware—note your fear. And be aware that you've let someone else stimulate you through his mouth and body. If you don't

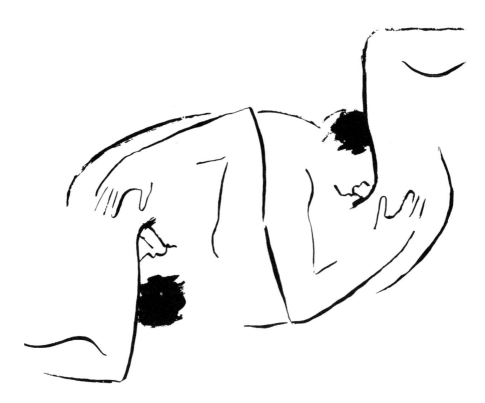

want this, don't let it continue; switch to something else. If you do want it, talking will help. Tell him you feel uneasy. Often it turns out the person was afraid of coming too soon, or felt like he was hogging all the attention. Getting upset like this isn't a glaring fault or a horrible failure, but a part of being human. Problems are normal just like good times. Being yourself, opening up to your bad parts as well as good, will encourage others to be themselves too, and can lead you to new levels of sharing, growing, and being.

Also, unless you want to have a standard passive/active couples role with your partner, where one always sucks and the other always gets sucked, you'll have to work on sharing control, and directing activity. This is a beautiful equalizing factor. It's a great challenge and also a great potential in the gay relationship.

Thrusting

So far I've been talking about fellatio where one person lays back and gets sucked off. There's another kind too, where one person slides his penis in and out of his friend's mouth. The Romans really liked this kind of fellatio, and called it *irrumatio*. It gives a different experience to the

person being fellated, because he's the one moving. He's more tense and active, he's controlling his experience much more so than in the other style, and he's moving his penis in an action called *thrusting*, which in itself can be a different and enjoyable sensation.

If you and your partner want to try this, have him lie down on his back with a pillow under his head. Then you straddle him with your hands and knees so that your crotch is over his face, and your head is above his. Move around until you can easily fit your penis into his mouth. He should make his mouth wet and form a snug ring with his lips around your shaft, as he'd do for the sliding action described earlier. He should suck on your penis, and otherwise keep still.

Now you want to slide your penis in and out. This thrusting is learned, and the only way to learn is by doing. Without moving your knees or using your hands, *move your penis with your hips.* Ask him to be patient and just experiment. Ask yourself, how in the world can I get myself to move in and out, and try out your muscles. Imagine a point at the base of your penis, and you want to cause this point to push out and up through your penis, and then pull back again. Everyone free of paralysis can do thrusting, if they want to. Just take your time and explore. Follow your sensations—see what feels good and do it again. Having an experienced guide or helper can be very useful too.

That's basically all there is to it. You can add things like rocking your pelvis from side to side or circularly (called "grinding"). Or your partner can rock his head from side to side, or move it up and back to meet your strokes, or use his tongue if he likes. Also, there are lots of different positions, standing, kneeling, and so on. Many couples like to work out their own ways. I'm saying, here are possibilities; there you are—explore, take what you want, and enjoy!

Some people can get into this second kind of fellatio, others don't like it. A frequent complaint is that the mouth-partner felt abused, that he had no control and the other thrust too deeply or violently, causing gagging, fear, or other troubles. This needn't happen if the two people can talk freely, and respect their own and each other's wants and needs. You might be able to work something out with the following suggestions:

—*Awareness:* if you're thrusting, you can be aware of your friend's comfort level, and with a little care, regulate the depth and strength of your thrusts.

—*Pausing:* try pausing for a moment between thrusts.

—*The Stopper Technique:* if your friend is thrusting in your mouth, you can have some control by wrapping one hand around his lower shaft, to use as a stopper, allowing only as much in as you like. If your hand is at the base, this also adds a pleasurable pressure against his body. You (or your partner) can use the hand to masturbate the lower part of his penis as the top part slides in and out, moving the hand down to the base as the penis slides in.

—*Mutuality:* in irrumation, the mouth-partner is likely to get bored, and this contributes a lot to feeling abused. There are some positions that allow mutual fondling, where he can caress you, and in others the mouth-partner can masturbate himself.

Sixty-Nine

Sixty-nine is mutual fellatio, the two of you sucking each other at the same time. It's called sixty-nine because the body positions are like the number 69. There are two positions. In the first, one person lies flat on his back and his friend kneels over him, head to feet. From here, you both can roll over on your sides to form the other.

The special delight of sixty-nine comes from the mutuality, doubling pleasure and warmth—it's an equal sharing, feeling the same joys, given to each other, at the same time, in the same position, at a very intimate level.

You can even go deeper with simultaneous orgasms, coming at the same time—but a cautionary note: this takes some care. Mutual orgasm can be meaningful, or also a confusing hangup. When people get really excited, toward orgasm, they tend to lose control and awareness. But sucking takes some attention and care. So, sucking and coming may not always mix well. As people have said, "What being done to me distracts me from what I'm doing."

You'll have to work this out for yourself. My opinion is, it's no big deal; it's nice to come together, and it's nice if we don't. Some couples like sixty-nine to simultaneous orgasms, and make it because they've learned to "fit" together. Other couples try hard but miss the point because they pay too much attention to the simultaneity and not enough to themselves. Getting orgasms together is not usually an easy thing.

Some people like to do sixty-nine for a while, and then alternate with one person and then the other resting. Others like to suck each other alternately until very turned-on, and then finish off with a sixty-nine. For myself, I find that mutual orgasm is nice, but I usually can't suck and be sucked at the same time for very long. So I might have sixty-nine for a while and then switch to other things. You can experiment, and see what happens. Also, if you feel relaxed, sixty-nine is a good way to work on problems like gagging.

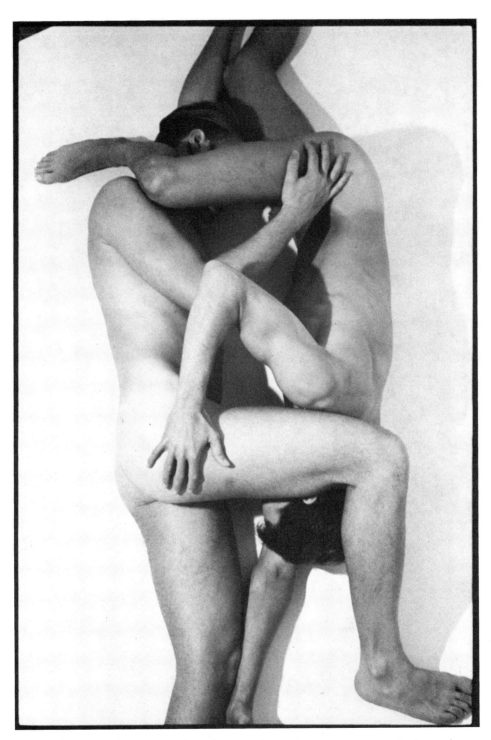

Making love via 69ing can be done in several positions. One of them is shown here.

5

ANAL INTERCOURSE

"Buggery is no sinne."

—*Rev. John Wilson*, 17th century English clergyman,
forced to resign for fucking three of
his male parishioners and a mare

*   *   *

Aug. 7, 1911: "I to meet enormous at 9. Will suck and take too."
May 13, 1911: "Millar into me."
May 14, 1911: "Into Millar . . . Imagine!"

—from the Diary of *Sir Roger David Casement* (1864–1916),
Irish revolutionary

*   *   *

The Malekulians said that a boy's penis grew large and strong by his being sodomized by the older male . . .

—*Melanesian cultural tradition*

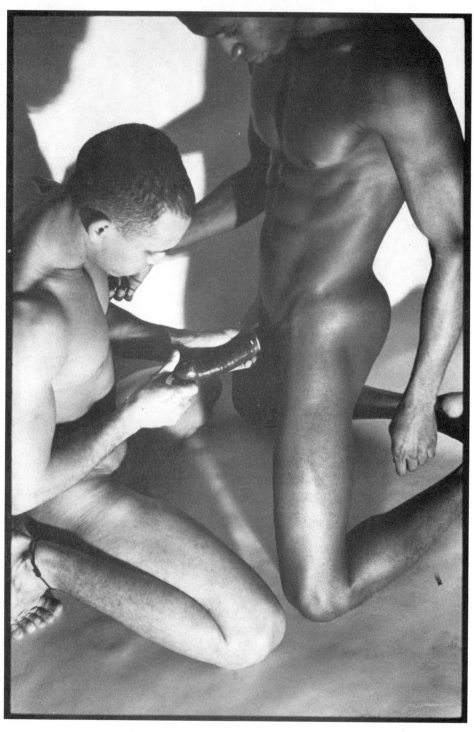

A condom should always be used in anal intercourse. Here one young man, who has just put a condom on his friend, admires the result.

ANAL INTERCOURSE

This is the chapter about two friends sharing penis and ass in sensual pleasure, where the penis slides in and out of the ass. This is called ass fucking, humping, buggering, sodomizing, and anal intercourse. For those who think sodomy is an offbeat or minor act, you'll be surprised to hear that actually it's been the most common and popular gay male sexual activity. All kinds of "simple" creatures, like bulls, frogs, guppies, dogs and so on, can frequently be seen making male–male sexual advances. For those animals that mount from behind (which include the amphibians and mammals, for example), this naturally leads to male–male mounting. These actions are usually simple and don't end in intercourse, though one or both partners may appear to get excited. But in some of the "higher" animals such as monkeys, complex activities are seen. That baboons do it often, seemingly to the point of orgasm, has become common knowledge. These acts usually involve an older and younger male and may develop into an ongoing relationship. The same is seen in macaque monkeys, where we have a description, for example, of a friendship between an adult and younger male that "was accompanied by frequent sodomy, mutual embracing, and social protection of the young animal by his full-grown partner." Sometimes relations will happen between nearly equal males, as noticed in squirrel monkeys. For our closest relatives, the chimps and gorillas, no observations are recorded, although among that unusually complex animal the porpoise, attempts at homosexual intercourse have been seen.

These behaviors suggest a phylogenetic pattern, in which anal intercourse became increasingly important through the evolution of animal life. In the simpler animals, sodomy happens by random chance, while in highly evolved social animals, it is often purposeful to that society. Thus ass fucking, as an aspect of nature, contains meaning and mystery of the life-spirit. When humankind came along, the pleasurable and mystical powers of sodomy could be cultivated on new levels, equal to our consciousness and intelligence.

History

The earliest records of our western "civilization" show that anal intercourse was important culturally and spiritually. It was tied up with worship of androgynous gods, who were part male and part female. When culture reached the point of having temples, there were special priests who acted as go-betweens for a person and the god, using anal intercourse as the medium. This intercourse was considered spiritually cleansing and uplifting, a sharing between person and god "held to be pure and fraternal," an act "venerable and holy." This was a common opinion throughout the ancient Mideast. Sometimes descriptions survive of sodomist relations among gods themselves, as for example the Egyptians Set and Horus.

Of course anal intercourse was not limited by any means to the spiritual level only. It was always seen as a form of pleasure and recreation. "Profane" sodomy (sex for its own sake) was, as the Bible continually reminds us, "rampant." Paradoxically enough, it was even "quite common if not customary" among the ancient Jews themselves, even though they started the taboos against it. Myth imputes the destruction of Sodom to this act (although most modern scholars now think Sodom was a morality story about the violation of hospitality rules, having nothing to do with sex).

Among the ancient Greeks, gayness was a part of everyday life. Anal intercourse was the common mode for men, and was considered an enjoyable, healthy, and uplifting activity. Being sensual and fun, it was done with humor (as were all pleasures to the Greeks) and called in slang "the carnal assault," the two partners described as "dog modest" (referring to the most popular position, that of rear entry).

Also it formed part of the morality of the state, the "proper" way to bring up young men and be an upstanding citizen. In Greek philosophy, education was conducted through the love between teacher and student, called *paiderastia*, and "by Paiderastia a man propagated his virtues, as it were, in the youth he loved, implanting them by the act of intercourse." We find this idea of virtue-giving through anal intercourse to be frequent in different cultures. In fact, at times a man was not considered to be living up to community standards unless he did practice sodomy:

> Lycurgus, the Spartan legislator, living some centuries before Socrates, refused the title of a good and deserving citizen to any man who had not a [male] friend that served him as a concubine.

To say that anal intercourse was practiced widely by the Greeks and, later, the Romans would probably be an understatement:

Who does not know that the Greeks and Romans were intrepid pedicons and determined cinedes? In the Greek and Latin authors . . . the male Venus parades on every page. . . . all burnt with the same fire, the common people, the higher classes, the king.

Pedicon was the Latin name for "a man who exercises his member in the anus." He was also called a *pederast* or *drawk*. The man "who allows himself to be invaded in this way" was called the *cinede (cinaedus)*, or *patient, catamite, minion, effeminate*. Also, if the cinede was an adult or "worn out," he was called an *exolete*.

The Romans didn't give the same moral and institutional values to anal intercourse as the Greeks did, but their ardor for it appears equal, none the less. Plenty of poets spoke of it, praising it, mocking well-known friends (with humor), spreading rumors and giving advice. Here are a few examples:

Stretch the foot and take your course, fly with soles in the air, with supple thighs, and nimble buttocks and libertine hands . . .
—Petronius "Arbiter" (d. 66 A.D.)

Caesar, the husband of all women, and the wife of all husbands.
—Curio the Elder (d. 53 B.C.)

Catching me with a boy, you harass me with your cries, and you tell me, my wife, that you have posteriors too.
Many and many a time did Juno say the same to Jupiter the Thunderer; yet he continued to sleep with slender Ganymede.
—Martial (40?-102 A.D.)

He was very much given to the intercourse between men, and amongst such he preferred men of ripe age, exoletes.
—Suetonius (*ca*. 70–*post* 122 A.D.) speaking of the Roman Emperor Galba (ruled 68–69 A.D.)

For you, ungrateful boy, I keep my treasures all, and no one shall enjoy them but yourself; my penis is growing: while it used to measure seven inches, now it measures ten.
—Pacificus Maximus, *Elegy II*, to Ptolemy

Overall, the ancients thought differently about sexual matters than we do. They lacked that guilt, that righteousness, that disgust of pleasure that the early Christians so treasured. In other words, they simply enjoyed it.

The general attitude of the Greeks, Romans, and other Mediterranean peoples towards anal intercourse can be summed up in the words of an ancient Greek historian, Timaeus, as he comments on a neighboring country:

> It is not considered objectionable among the Tyrrhenians [of Italy] to have to do with boys openly, whether actively or passively, for paederasty [man/youth love] is a custom of the country. . . . They pay homage to love. . . . they are very fond of women, but find more pleasure with boys and young men. . . .

All this changed with the rise of the Christian church, which took a harsh Jewish creed and made it more harsh. Sexual matters were far from perfect in the ancient Mediterranean world (especially as regards the rights of women), but there is a vast gulf between arguing the pros and cons of passive sodomy and condemning all sodomy as against God's will. Christianized Roman emperors such as Justininan were afraid that God would cause earthquakes and fires like he did on Sodom if homosexuality were not wiped out. And many early Christians believed that all sex was sinful (some even going so far as to castrate themselves), thus making gay sex doubly evil.

Male gayness was common in all Europe, even before the advent of Christianity, and it seems likely anal intercourse was widely practiced. At least this was true for the Celts of France, according to the Roman Athenaeus:

> The Celts take more pleasure in pederastia than any other Nation, to such a degree that amongst them it is no rarity to find a man lying between two minions.

Many references tell how common ass fucking was among the Normans, who conquered England in 1066. As to England itself, Anselm, writing to Archdeacon William in 1102, says, "This sin has been so public that hardly anyone has blushed for it, and many, therefore, have plunged into it without realizing its gravity." The fortunes of sodomy rose and fell during the Middle Ages depending on religious and social feelings. Sometimes you could be more open about it, and sometimes you were burned at the stake. Sodomy was a potent crime against God, and accusation of it was often used to punish political enemies. Thus, for example, the Knights Templar, famous during the Crusades, were accused of sodomy in order to remove their political power.

Three soldiers. Etching. Illustration from *Juliette*
by the Marquis de Sade

Different European states held different attitudes on the matter. Offi-
cially it was condemned everywhere, but practically speaking the countries varied in tolerance. Especially after the Renaissance it seems that
sometimes matters would be more open. For example, the Scot Lithgow
reports in 1610 while touring Italy:

> for beastly Sodomy, it is as rife here [in Padua] as in Rome, Naples,
> Florence, Bullogna, Venice, Ferrara, Genoa, Parma not being ex-
> empted, nor yet the smallest village of Italy: A monstrous filthinesse, and
> yet to them a pleasant pastime, making songs, and singing Sonnets of
> the beauty and pleasure of their Bardassi, or buggered boyes.

Of a later time, one scholar writes,

> If we may trust to Aloysia Sigaea, the Italians and Spaniards did it;
> also the Dutchmen, with whom towards the middle of the XVIIIth Cen-
> tury, as J. David Michaelides tells us . . . this habit was so much in
> vogue, that the punishment of death was hardly of avail against it; also
> the Parisians. . . .

The Mideast was not only the cradle of western civilization but also
of those cultures which today embrace North Africa, Turkey, all the near
East, India and Indonesia. Male gayness was very widespread in these cultures, at times to the point of rivalling heterosexual values and institutions.
Having been bypassed, so to speak, by the accusing finger of the Judeo-
Christian god, gayness in these lands continued to flourish as it had in ancient times.

In the geographical center of the Mideast lies Persia, modern Iran.
During the middle and early modern ages, Persia flourished as a center
of religious, philosophical and artistic thought. And the general code of
law and customs,

> including one of the most ancient of Malthusian laws seeking popula-
> tion control, fostered sodomy in social and theological practice. Thus,
> Persians became one of the first of endemically and customarily inverted
> peoples.

"True love" for males in Persia was often gay in nature, and poets,
philosophers, holy men praised it, using its feelings to enrich their thinking, and vice versa. Thus sodomy was connected with "higher" virtues,
and anal intercourse became a way of reaching new spiritual levels and
of teaching the young, just as it was with the Greeks.

Much was written on the joys of sodomy. Muhammad ibn Malik, an
Arabic poet of the twelfth century in Andalusia, wrote the following poem:

FACING MECCA

Friday
     in the mosque
my gaze fell upon a slim young man
     beautiful
as the rising moon.

When he bent forward in prayer
my only thought was
                    oh to have him
stretched out
            flat before me,
butt-up,
face-down.

And Ubaid'i Zakani (d. 1371), another Arab poet, wrote the following poem in humorous vein:

. . . when he had undone the cord of his drawers
He knelt down, the illustrious warrior.
Then Hamun displayed a pillar as formidable as a monster
    of legend,
And, as his ancestors taught him, plunged it . . .
And now it was Hamun's turn to submit.
The vigorous Rustam, that most valiant champion . . .

Bearing these many wounds, the two contestants
Had earned their place among the mightiest warriors.
Thou, too, my little brother, like some great champion,
Wilt be well advised, I assure thee,
To lie prone, with rump held high . . .

In India it was said, "The worth of slit the Hindoo knows, the worth
of hole the Moslem chose." In Egypt, "the epithet *el-fa'eel* (sodomite) could
be safely affixed to a goodly number of Egyptian names." And, according to Riza Bey, in Turkish baths it "is not only frequent in practice, but
is largely accepted as normal," adding that Easterners "love to eat both
figs (anus) and pomegranates (cunnus)!"

My prickle is big and the bathboy spoke:
"thrust fiercely up fundament with lionlike stroke!"
Said I: "It won't fit!" Then he: "What a joke!
I've had some hashish!" So I battered his poke.

Throughout these countries, youth, beauty, and ass fucking were in-
tertwined in social custom and institutions, such as that of the male belly-
dancer: "As dancing boys they [sodomites] obsessed nearly every Eastern

potentate, and they were found writhing in nearly every bazaar." Many rulers and high government officials kept boys and/or eunuchs, as for example, the famous Saladin of Crusader times, who was questioned on the matter:

> When King Richard the Lion-Hearted jestingly asked Sultan Saladin which he preferred, girls or boys, the Sword of Islam solemnly replied: "Girls? Allah forbid! It's as if you were to serve me leg of lamb without the bone!"

A rather sexist Arabian folk saying was:

The penis smooth and round,
    Was made with anus for to fit;
It would look just like a hatchet
    Were it made for sake of slit.

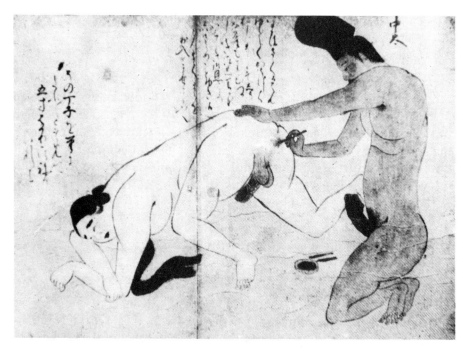

From the Catamites' Scroll, dated 1321. Sambo-in temple, Daigo, Japan

In North Africa, not only was sodomy prevalent among the Egyptians, but also with the Berbers, Moors, and other Arabs. And in Afghanistan, a typical greeting was, "May the devil rub thy buttocks, yah Huzoor!" In the same region lived the Pathans, whose pederastic love song (*Zekhmi Dil*, "Wounded Heart") went:

There's a boy across the river with a bottom like a peach,
And I have to get to him!
There's a boy lives there that loves me, and he's *almost* in my reach,
But I don't know how to swim!

His bottom hides a precious pouch that's lined with Persian silk
with gold threads on the rim.
I want to pour within it pearls and opals white as milk;
I have to get to him! . . .

> from "Afghani Love Song," version by Edward A. Lacey
> (*Gay Roots* vol. 2, Gay Sunshine Press, 1993)

In Libya anal intercourse was known as *el-dudeh* ("the worm"), while in Hindu culture the "active" partner was called *gandhmara* ("anus beater"). In Hindu society, anal intercourse was usually frowned upon, as was gayness in general. But as I noted before, this was more the attitude of the upper class and intelligentsia, the "lower" classes being more relaxed, because the god Shiva had had sodomy with other gods. We do not know how prevalent this kind of sex was there, except that it was at least fairly popular. The nomadic tribes living on the middle plains of Asia —the Turanians, Cossacks, Huns, Tartars, Mongols, Turkomans, Yakuts and others—practiced "flagrant sodomy," the Elizabethan Samuel Purchas noting that the Tartars were "addicted" to it.

Gayness was also historically widespread and held in esteem in China. Again, anal intercourse was the popular mode, and was referred to in Chinese literature as "sharing the peach." This phrase arose out of the first recorded instance of sodomy in Chinese history:

Duke Ling [around 500 B.C.] committed sodomy with a young court official, Mi Tzu-hsia, who had a face "as pretty as that of a blooming maiden." . . . One day, when the two of them were sauntering hand in hand in the Duke's Eastern Garden, Mi playfully picked a ripe peach from a tree. After having a few bites himself, he unceremoniously pushed the remaining part of the peach into Duke Ling's mouth. In those days, such an act was considered one of great disrespect for the head of a state. And yet Duke Ling gladly munched the peach and said aloud: "This peach tastes so good because it has been in your mouth first."

Nobles, courtiers and even emperors engaged in sodomy, this being especially prevalent during the Manchu dynasty (17th–20th centuries). Relations were most common between men and youths. One of the classic erotic masterpieces of world literature, the *Chin P'ing Mei*, involves the hero, Hsi-men, in this scene:

> Hsi-men opened the boy's robe, pulled down his pants, and gently stroked his penis. . . . while the boy surrendered his bottom to a mighty warrior, Hsi-men stroked his stiff penis. . . . Said the boy: "He pushed his poker so violently between my buttocks that today they are swollen with great pain. When I asked him to stop, he pushed his poker in and out all the more."

In both China and Japan, male prostitution was widespread, and "a thriving and honorable profession" sanctified in China by Tcheou-wang, God of Sodomy, and in Japan consecrated in male Geisha houses. In China, "the boys were made to sit on benches made of boxwood sprigs in graduated sizes, in order to prepare them to welcome the pleasures expected of them." In both cultures these prostitutes could still be found on special streets as late as the last world war.

The majority of "primitive" cultures on all continents and throughout human history sanctioned some form of male gayness. As one scholar noted, "anal coitus is the usual technique employed by male homosexuals in preliterate societies."

These relationships would take on a variety of forms, depending on social customs. One common form involves a marriage between a man and a transvestite, who may also be a magician. Here, the transvestite usually takes the "passive" role with his husband, though in some cultures he is allowed to take female wives in addition. Such customs have been noted among diverse peoples, such as the Chuckchee of Siberia, the Aleuts and Konyages of Alaska, the Creek and Omaha of the U.S., "the negro population of Zanzibar," and the Bangala of the upper Congo. Sometimes transvestites sold their favors, as in the Inca Empire:

> The last which was taken, and which fought most courageously, was a man in the habite of a woman, which confessed that from a childe he had gotten his living by that filthinesse, for which I caused him to be burned.
> —Nuno de Guzmán, at Cuzco, 1530.

Another common custom united boys or youths with somewhat older men, sometimes in temporary marriages, sometimes as part of initiation rites, and at other times simply as a form of love-making. For example,

> Among many of the aborigines of Australia this type of coitus is a recognized custom between unmarried men and uninitiated boys. Strehlow writes of the Aranda as follows: "Pederasty is a recognized custom. . . . Commonly a man, who is fully initiated but not yet married, takes a boy of ten or twelve years old, who lives with him as a wife for several years, until the older man marries."

Oftentimes anal intercourse is thought to "strengthen" a boy or impart manhood to him, as in the following:

> Keraki bachelors of New Guinea universally practice sodomy, and in the course of his puberty rites each boy is initiated into anal intercourse by the older males. . . . This practice is believed by the natives to be necessary for the growing boy. . . . The Kiwai have a similar custom.

This attitude corresponds to that among the ancient Greeks and Persians. And then there are such societies as that of the Siwans of western Egypt:

> Among the Siwans of Africa, for example, all the men and boys engage in anal intercourse. They adopt the feminine role only in strictly sexual situations and males are singled out as peculiar if they do not indulge in these homosexual activities. Prominent Siwan men lend their sons to each other, and they talk about their masculine love affairs as openly as they discuss their love of women. Both married and unmarried males are expected to have both homosexual and heterosexual affairs.

Usually in these cultures, a man is not exclusively homosexual, though he may have homosexual relations throughout most of his life.

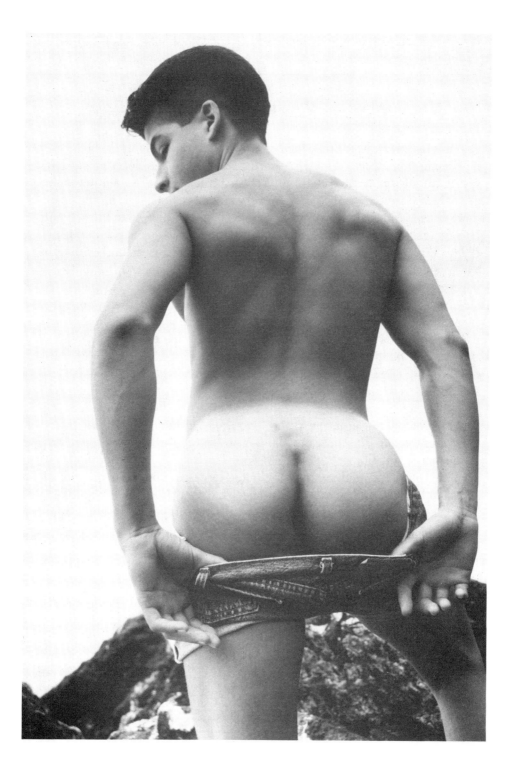

The sexual practices described in this chapter should be performed in a safe-sex way (see p. 37 for guidelines). A latex condom should *always* be used in anal intercourse (see pp. 30–31 for correct usages of condoms).

Techniques

Let me say right off that the best way to learn anal intercourse is to do it. Keep in mind that the ways of sharing sex must be developed; they don't spring fully formed into the mind. Yet the basic actions of the intercourse are easy and simple, as they are for every kind of sex. That is, all the necessary information is already in you; you need only learn how to bring it out, to overcome any confusions and develop rapport with your partner(s). It's the prohibitions, the guilts and complexities in our society and each of us that prevents us knowing and doing what we want. Again, it's a matter of good consciousness, feeling relaxed, and wanting to explore, to get into it.

Anal intercourse involves two people, who between them create the pleasures. At any one time, one person will have his penis in the other's ass; this may be reversed later on. One or both (or at certain times neither) persons will be moving. In the anal intercourse I will discuss, both partners want to engage in it, and they cooperate with each other. There's no such thing as a "passive" and an "active" role; there is no dominant and no submissive—these are false labels put on us by hostile outsiders. Ass fucking is an act of creation where two are together. There is vast flexibility in who can do what, but there is no "one up/one down" mentality unless you want that.

So, you want to know how to do it? Here it is: you kneel on your elbows and knees, and relax your ass such that your body *wants* to take in your friend's erect penis. He kneels directly behind your rear end, facing your way. He bends over you, guiding his lubricated penis to your anus-opening, and then gently pushes it inside as you draw it in. Then he causes his penis to slide up and down inside by thrusting his hips back and forth, while you keep still or rotate your hips in a side-to-side motion.

That's basically it. From the description, you might think the penis-person is having all the fun. That's not true. The ass-person may be enjoying even more pleasure. There are two reasons for this: the anus is very sensitive to erotic touch, like the lips; and the inserted penis will massage a small gland behind the testicles, called the prostate. When this gland is touched during sexual arousal, the pleasurable feelings are multiplied in intensity. Thus, during anal intercourse, powerful erotic feelings can flow all through the body around the genitals, anus, and internal organs; the

rectum may begin contracting up and down in waves of pleasure, causing an anal orgasm along with the genital one.

The penis-person can masturbate his partner; the ass-person can masturbate himself, or he can even reach around to insert a finger in his partner's anus—many possibilities are open, for you to discover exactly what you like to do and enjoy, according to your different wants and moods.

In other words, if you're new to it, it's best to learn in steps and not expect to know or do everything at once; usually it takes months or years to feel and shape the many potential desires and satisfactions. The basic act is simple, but our culture teaches us to be so inhibited about sex, gay sex, and asses in particular that some confusion may have to be worked through.

Once over this, new levels of meaning will be open to you. The fun of sexual arousal and ejaculation is *recreational*, is entertainment. Loss of ego sense (sense of "I") and dissolving into another, when all thinking disappears and both your ecstasies merge together, is *affirmational*, is centering, growthful, spiritual. Wrapping your warm body around another, or to be so enfolded, with torso and legs, penis and ass, desire and care, feels good in describable and indescribable ways, to the life/spirit/me. And this is creative experience at its best.

Where to begin? by being candid with yourself, that you want to explore, and then finding a partner, a friend, a one-night stand, whatever.

You'll probably want to taste both roles, insertor and insertee: you might find one more meaningful for you, or you might like both.

I should mention here that all our explorations, indeed, any suggestions given in this book, are meant as enjoyable adventures, as good experiences. If anything turns into hard work, if you seem driven to ignore your sensuality, and speed on in haste instead, or get worried and upset, it's time to stop. To start over or talk to someone. You can't force love, it unfolds. Oftentimes things have to be learned, but if this is not enjoyable learning, it's probably not for you. Curiosity is your best bet here, and leave your seriousness at the door—sodomy is an extra, not a pain in the ass.

First, let me explain the basic positions and motions that go with them, then I'll discuss matters about the ass-person, then the penis-person. Let me go through each position, the motions that can be used, and its advantages and disadvantages; these, of course, can only be explained approximately, as people vary in what fits for them.

One position I've already described, with the ass-person crouching down to receive his friend from behind. The advantages are, easy and fairly deep entry, and freedom of movements. Those of the penis-person include *thrusting, grinding* (rotating the hips circularly as you'd do to play with a hoola-hoop), *rocking* (turning the pelvis from left to right), and body motions like swaying from the knees. These motions allow different experiences for both partners. Those of the ass-person include *complementary-thrusting* (the same as for the penis-person, except that your timing and his are slightly off), *counter-thrusting* (where you push as he pulls), grinding or rocking as he thrusts, and body movements. All these motions are easy to learn, once you feel safe enough to try them and someone can help you a little.

The disadvantages of this position are both people having to hold themselves up (getting tired and not having free hands), the penis not pressing too much against the prostate, and not being face to face (if that's important to you).

A variation on this position has the ass-person lying flat on his stomach (with his hips raised a little on a pillow if you like). This allows him to relax more and he has his hands free to do whatever. The penis-person lies on top and thus also can be more relaxed and have free hands. However, penetration is not as easy and you can't thrust as deeply. Also, the ass-person is weighed down and restricted in how he can move, though the penis-person can still move freely.

From this position, both partners can roll over on their sides, still facing the same way, with one leg drawn up. This position allows bodily relaxation plus free hands to explore and caress. Also entry is easy and fairly deep, and avoids the one person pressing fully on his friend. Movements are somewhat limited, though vigorous thrusting is still easy once you get used to the posture.

An interesting variation on this position has both partners on their sides, but facing each other. Here the penis-person must extend his pelvis between the other's bent legs. This position allows deep entry and a full massage of the prostate. Also the hands and mouths are free, and movement is fairly easy once insertion is made.

Then there is the full-front position, in which the ass-person lies on his back, drawing his knees up to his chest and over the shoulders of the penis-person, who presses down on him face to face (a pillow can be put under the pelvis to raise it even higher, or the penis-person can push back his friend's feet over his head). This position allows for easy penetration and very deep entry, a good massage of the prostate, plus full movements by the penis-person. However, the ass-person can't move much, though his hands are free.

Another favorite position is a standing one, in which both friends stand up, facing the same way, and the ass-person bends over at the waist, using a wall, table, or other support. This can also be done on the knees rather than the feet, say, at the edge of the bed. If both partners are not of the same height at the waist, some adjustment will have to be made. This position is convenient to use outdoors, and allows easy penetration and full movements, if something solid is around to hold on to.

These are the basic positions; many others are also possible. Each is different, and may vary for you in feelings and emotional meaning. You might be specially thrilled by thrusting from behind, wrapping around his backside, stroking his chest and stomach with your hand. Or your love to unite may reach out strongest with him entering you face to face, snug and kissing deeply.

Fears of Being Entered

I've already mentioned some of the pleasures possible through receiving the penis in intercourse. Now let's talk about how you do it, and things you might be afraid of.

This matter is simply put: your rectum can receive a large penis easily and fully, and this can be quite pleasurable, if you want it. And *you must want it*, before it can happen. That is, you must be at ease, in mind and body. The rectum is like a very elastic pipe with a set of muscular rings at the end, the anus. The anus acts as a plug, to stop things from going out, or

to let them in. It tightens and relaxes like purse-strings on a bag, and is fairly strong.

This muscle is controlled by the mind, and emotions influence how tense it will be at any given time. Good fucking can't happen unless the anus is relaxed, and this may take some learning.

Many of us are taught to be ashamed of our rear ends, of the things that happen there, and the sensations of this area. The anus can be an erotic place; most children experience pleasure in shitting, but many adults ignore these feelings, in their rush to get the act over with as little guilt as possible. The rear end becomes an ignored and mysterious place. The anus is usually held tight, and becomes the site of problems like hemorrhoids.

Yet the feelings are still there. Awareness and conscious control of the anus can be learned, although this takes time to discover.

Look at it as exploring something new, part of your own body. The first thing is, how you feel about your anus and rectum. Are they a part of you, or do you emotionally push them away? If you feel bad about your ass, that it's a dirty place, this is where your explorations must begin.

Explore your anus, to discover how it feels and that it's not dirty, that you can touch it and not get hurt. You can do this two ways: by yourself and/or with a friend.

If you explore yourself you have control over your actions. Climb into a tub of hot water (or a shower or on your bed) and relax. Then with your fingertips explore your genitals and thighs, gliding around to feel what it's like. Then bend your legs and slide your fingers down between them, lower and deeper, past your testicles. Touch your anus very lightly with one finger. Then with several. Push down a little—how does it feel? If you like that, try masturbating while pressing several fingers on your ass.

Now you've made contact. If it feels good there or if you sense that it will, keep exploring. Don't push yourself to do more than you want at any one time—pace yourself comfortably. But try to tune in on your rear; discover when it's tight and when it's loose, and how you can control this.

At some point you'll want to take the plunge, inserting a finger inside. It's a remarkable discovery, that you can do this, and opens up a world of new sensations. Be aware that the rectum is a sturdy, flexible organ and can't be hurt by fingers, a penis or other similar objects, unless you violently intend to do so: if you don't make your finger force your ass, or your ass force your finger, they will work well together. Sharp edges like fingernails can scratch it, and that's not too good, so trim your nail a little first. But if it can take all your excrement, it can take smaller things like fingers and cocks.

Usually there's nothing inside the end-part of the rectum; but sometimes there might be small particles. You'll discover that these are harmless and easily washed off after. Or you can clean out your rectum first, douching with an enema bottle and warm water. Many men who enjoy ass fucking do this. Or you can use a quick and easy method developed by Dr. Bill Horstman, a San Francisco sexologist, which consists of douching with a large basting syringe, which can be bought at most supermarkets. It's a big plastic tube, pointed at one end (make sure to file down the tip so it's not scratchy) and with a rubber bulb on the other. Filled with water, it holds just enough to clean the rectum thoroughly and simply.

Now, I suggest you lie back on your bed (or wherever), and bend your legs to bring your feet up close to your rear. Get into an enjoyable masturbation with one hand, and grease a finger of the other with KY or another lubricant. Then place it at your anus, and push very gently, slowly. Your finger will go in just a little. If you want to get your finger in farther, you must keep pushing gently and firmly, and release the anus muscle. Then you will feel your finger go all the way through, past the thick muscle and into the soft, quiet rectum.

It may feel uncomfortable at first, because you've taught yourself to regard anything in the rectum as dark and dirty, and you'll want to push it out. But take it easy; try letting your finger rest there as you're masturbating. You may feel a little burning or irritation, but this will turn to pleasure if your masturbation is feeling good. If you like, climax with your finger inside, and see how it feels. If all this seems good to you, keep up the exploration. If it bothers you, withdraw and try again later; take your time.

Once you get used to your finger inside, you can discover new things. Stick your finger all the way in. Then feel around inside, gently, as you masturbate, until you touch on a silver-dollar sized, round lump behind your testicles. This is your prostate gland, and you'll know when you've touched it because it'll feel hard and nice. If there's a sharp pain, however, withdraw your finger and go see a doctor, because it means your prostate might be infected.

But otherwise, try moving your finger up and down against the prostate as you masturbate. This will probably feel very good. Also you'll notice that you can squeeze and unsqueeze your anus around the finger.

Now you'll want to learn to loosen it enough to let in larger sizes. It may seem at first like your anus has a separate personality, doing things in its own way. But this is only because you've separated it in your mind. If you get to know it better, it'll eventually make friends with you, and the separation will disappear. After using your finger to meet it, get to know your anus more intimately. You can trace warm wet rings around its outside; after inserting a finger you can massage it, pressing outward in a circle, tensing and calming it, trying to curl your finger around its side, feeling its touch through the skin—while exploring, if you act like you're shitting, pushing out, this will help even more. Practice stretching and tensing/calming your anus around your finger; you want to do this until it can be widened easily and painlessly.

Next you can insert two (or more) fingers, seeing how far you can bend them apart. Later, you might want to try a dildo (a straight, smooth, round tipped object like those found in sex shops). It's a good idea to use something that won't break, such as plastic or rubber. Glass objects can sometimes shatter, and a candle could snap in the middle, leaving half stuck inside. So be careful. Otherwise feel free to indulge, since you can only hurt your rectum with sharp objects or violent jabbing motions.

Or you might want to move right on to experimenting with a friend. And this is also another way to learn about your ass. Say to him, "I'd sure like to enjoy anal pleasures, but I'm not used to it and a little afraid." Then your friend can turn you on: (after douching if necessary) he can place his fingers at your anus during sex. He can, if he likes, suck and tongue your anus, or insert his finger(s). These are called analingus and postillioning, and

can be soothing, warm, and exciting; they have their own sections at the end of this chapter. A nice thing is for your friend to masturbate you as his finger is inserted in your rectum.

If neither of you can get this far, because your anus just won't relax, it means you're anxious somewhere, or you simply don't know how to relax it yet. This is not always the easiest thing to learn, and there's no reason to feel bad about it, since the anus is very likely to just follow old habits of not opening up. It takes time. Take risks only when you really feel safe, and don't allow yourself to be forced open. It helps to talk about this, and how you're feeling.

One especially nice act that can relax your rear is for your friend, during sex, to simply trace soft rings around the opening, pressing with one or two lubricated fingertips, going around and around. This usually has a calming, whole-some effect.

If, after much gentle trying over a period of time, your anus just won't loosen, I would suggest you might have a mental wish not to be entered, that you aren't aware of. If this might be, explore the possibility in your mind and with your friend; you may want to see a counselor or sexologist, or you may decide that anal intercourse just isn't for you.

If you do progress in your explorations, the time will come for your friend to insert his penis. If this is what you both want, let it happen as it will, without planning on doing it. Be easy about it, trying one of the positions I've described. It may take several (or many) tries, so relax and feel the sensations. If it hurts, and it might, just ask him to withdraw gently. Some pain may happen, and this is usually OK. If it's a strong or sharp pain, back off, but you'll discover that the mild pain turns to blissful delight during sex. As he enters, you may experience a violent urge to go to the bathroom, or you may imagine you're going to piss or shit right there. This is a fantasy of your mind and body, through lack of use and conditioning; if you respect these feelings and have patience, they will change through practice. Also, if you're sexually excited, these feelings and any tightness will lessen considerably. The best rule is to take it in steps, going easy and smooth. It may seem difficult for a while, but you may be surprised by a rapid change from discomfort to sweet pleasure.

There is a special position for you if you want to take entire control of the act. This way you can go fast or slow as you like. It involves your friend lying on his back. Then you squat down over his hips, facing him, and guide his penis to your ass. Then you simply sit down on it, gently and as far as you want to go. You make any motions with your hips, or you can just feel what it's like.

There are two other ways you can take more control, which are useful

not only if you're new at it, but also if he has an extra large penis. You can use your hand as a stopper, wrapping it around his penis where you like so only so much is let in (or he can use his own hand). Also you can use a position allowing only limited entry—a good one is where you lie flat on your stomach, with him lying on top; by pushing down with your pelvis or tightening your buttocks you can limit penetration even more.

After insertion, give a luxurious amount of time in becoming used to it. Let him worry about what to do, and you just pay attention to the warmth and sensualness of it. Try masturbating—this is a regular part of the intercourse, and may surprise you with its intensity.

Enjoyment in being the ass-person comes with letting go into the experience. It's not being passive in our cultural sense, since he can be lying still with you making all the motions. Rather it's receiving and giving, his care and yours, your bodily/emotional desires and his, in various combinations. It's reaching and creating with your excitement, so that your union becomes fusion of give and take, in and out—a greater wholeness of being.

You can be entirely still or jumping all over, or anywhere in between. Most of the body motions are easy to learn, such as thrusting and grinding. It can get a little complicated at times, however, since if you both move your motions must be coordinated. The easiest thing to do is rotate your rear in a circular way, as he thrusts. A tricky and subtle skill is to learn how to squeeze your anus, tight and loose, to fondle his pleasure more and start vibrating, glowing ripples up and down your rectum. You'll know if you're moving in good ways, because you'll feel a rhythmic flow inside and out. You'll begin to forget where you are, as your movements melt into his.

Performance Fears

As with the ass-person, so too with the penis-person, being of good consciousness, open, wanting to explore and cooperate—with these, knowledge and pleasure come easy. Then, it's simply moving your body in tune with your pleasurable sensations; touching and rubbing in joyful ways. Once your penis is in his rectum, all this will tend to happen by itself; just let go and explore what feels good.

If you haven't done it before, you might feel clumsy, confused; body motions used in anal intercourse aren't used many places outside sex, so how can you be expected to know them instantly? If you feel uncomfortable, tell him you're exploring—maybe he can help you out.

One big worry is that you might be embarrassed, that you'll fail. This is called "performance anxiety:" you can't get it up, you can't keep it up, and/or you can't carry through to climax. The penis is sensitive to worry, like a barometer it goes up and down with anxiety level (among other things, such as fatigue). In other words, if you're too upset or too unsteady, it's pretty hard to fake it with your cock. And once you've "failed," it makes it even harder.

But actually, this penis-sensitivity can be seen as a good thing: it makes you be honest. There's a big difference between *performing* in intercourse, and *sharing*. I'm not writing about performance at all—if you want to put on a show, entertain your partner and prove your skills, go read something else because I'm not interested in it. If you want to *be* together, mixing *with* him, giving and taking as two growing people—then you'll want to be honest, clear, human, yourself. And then, if you go limp, you go limp. Big deal! That's part of being yourself at the time. You're scared, uncertain, confused; these are important feelings; don't deny them! People manage to get themselves into a fix by making things worse than they are. Worries in sex are common, human things; we all fail, including me your humble sexpert. By discovering you can just be you, wherever you're at during the moment, it won't matter so much; it'll be OK.

If you've tried before and failed a lot, you probably feel pretty bad about it. "I'm a loser; ain't it awful." Well, you'll never get over it with that attitude. What keeps people from doing what they want is "I *can't* do it; I'm super anxious that I'll just fail again." This vicious circle—failure, fear of failure—needs to be broken, and the first step is removing the emotional punch of "failing." Examine why you see your act as a failure; you must have had a goal in mind that you didn't reach, and this to you was bad. Why is this a bad thing? Try looking at it from a new point of view, seeing it neither as bad or good, but simply as an event which happened.

Find a friend who's willing to work on it with you, explaining that you want to do this, but couldn't manage it in the past. Then you can go on to break the cycle, by learning that you can enjoy yourself. This needs trust and help from your friend, as you learn together. First, you'll want to discover you can enjoy contact with his rear end. When you're having sex, try inserting your finger on or in his anus, and he into yours, especially at climax. Thus you'll discover you can give and get extra pleasure this way. After you're used to this, try the special position I mentioned before: you lie on your back, and your friend straddles you at the waist, to insert your penis in him. You don't have to move a thing; just relax and feel it. Often the person was so worried about what to do after insertion that he could never get that far.

Let your friend do all the movements. If you go limp, try again or switch to something else. Make sure it's OK with you and your friend if you go limp, since this (limp = failed = bad) can be the biggest part of feeling like you're no good. Take time discovering that you can be erect and be inside him. If it doesn't happen sooner or later, you may want to just let it rest until a better time.

After you feel comfortable being inside him, try moving. As you begin to do this, open up to your desires. Try the side-ways position, both facing the same way, since it won't be as demanding as some others. Once you feel fluid and relaxed mentally, your body will flow also. Flex it; try out your pelvis. Just move it around any old way and see what happens. You'll probably discover most if not all the possible movements. Thrusting is with the small of the back (just above your ass), making your pelvis tip up and down. You'll be rusty at first; practice makes better (dancing is also a good place to practice.).

You'll find you can move in ways that express your feelings: slow, fast, hard, soft, simple, complex, as you like. Also it'll take time to coordinate your movements with him; this cooperation is learned, as you pick up each other's styles and talk about what's good for you. If both of you are into moving at the same time, perhaps the easiest is for you to thrust while he rotates his pelvis. To do this try to draw an imaginary circle around your waist with your rear end. And then there's thrusting together—there are two ways to do it. As you push your penis deeper into his ass, he can push against you; and then pull away from you as you pull away from him. This is the *meeting style*. In the *rhythm style*, you both thrust at the same time; you make the exact same rhythm. Obviously this would never work, except that you and he don't move at exactly the same time: one of you is "off" slightly, pushing down a little after he pushes down, pulling up a little after, and so on.

There's another important matter that's good to know. And this is about forcing your friend's ass. There are two ways to have anal intercourse, as an inter-action, or as a game of force and selfish controlling between suspicious partners. Time and again, it is the good consciousness that matters; feeling warm, trusting, open with your friend. With this attitude, the problem of forced entry will never come up. But it often happens that a tight anus is rammed by a callous or overeager partner, and this is not good. As I've taken time to explain, the anus muscles will be as loose as the person feels. If the anus doesn't relax, intercourse can still happen, as the ass can be entered by sheer force. This is usually painful, and may hurt the ass-person by tearing the rectum. You will instantly know if you're being entered in a bad way, because it'll hurt a lot. And that's the time to stop things.

Be gentle when you enter another person: after you're in, you can use healthy stroking, but not at first; don't plunge in like a high diver. You

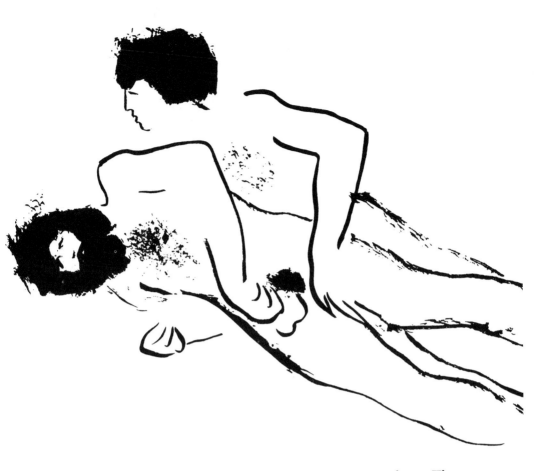

should slide in with a firm, easy pushing. If not, try again later. The anus may not be either totally relaxed or tight; it doesn't have to be gaping wide open—but if firm pressure doesn't work, don't go on. The best indicator of trouble is pain—a little is usually OK, especially if the ass-person is inexperienced, but a lot means *stop*. If the penis is really large, some extra stretching may be necessary, and this may take a little practice for the anus to get used to. You can insert your penis in just part way, and then withdraw, so that his anus will become adjusted to accept this amount. The anus is very flexible, but it may take some practice—try inserting a little, then full insertion later, followed by gentle movements and then finally moving as comfortable. This gradual approach, in many matters, is usually the safest and most secure way.

From all the foregoing, it may seem like anal intercourse is a very complex activity. But actually it's a simple thing, and comes easy with an easy mind. It's another way of sharing bodies and feelings, meeting and exploring the world of ourselves. It can be a way of pleasuring, growing, loving, a nice pastime or a meaty pursuit.

Postillioning

Postillioning is inserting a gloved finger (fingers) into the anus, and may include massaging it, the rectum, or/and the prostate gland inside. At its extreme, this can become fist fucking, which is insertion of the whole hand. I've already mentioned postillioning as a pleasant addition to the sex act, and also as a good preparation for anal intercourse. I'd like to explain in more detail how you can do it, and things to watch out for.

The index or middle finger is best used, being long and strong. The gloved finger must be well lubricated with spit or oil or vaseline (don't use anything with soap, as this will upset the rectal eco-system), and then placed at the anal opening. The outside can be caressed in circles and mild probes. This is usually a very warm experience and helps relax the area.

Make insertion by pressing gently and firmly inwards, wobbling the tip a little as necessary. On the one hand, your finger won't go in at all if the ass is as tight as it can be. On the other, if the anus is completely relaxed the finger will slide in with hardly any effort. Postillioning is a great way to help someone explore their rear and learn to loosen the anus-opening. Insertion is helped if the ass-person pushes lightly out as if going to the bathroom. You probably won't find anything inside the rectum, and whatever you do find will be harmless. If you must have him absolutely clean inside he can douche with an enema bottle and warm water.

Once inside, you'll feel the thick, strong, muscular ring which is the anus, and beyond it the soft side of the rectum. Keep at least your fingertip beyond the anus, or contraction of the muscle will cause the finger to pop out again. Once your finger is inside, you can explore around, pushing it in as far as it'll go, curling it around the anus, flicking it back and forth, finding the prostate gland. This gland makes the fluid for ejaculation, and can be found behind the testicles; if you stroke it during masturbation or fellatio, it feels great (if it hurts a lot instead, it's probably infected; if it doesn't feel like much of anything, you're probably nervous). If you insert two fingers, you can push them apart inside as a way to stretch and loosen the anus. Just having the finger(s) positioned inside while sucking or jacking-off is quite delightful, while sliding them up and down at ejaculation can double or quadruple the intensity. When it's time to finish, just pull the finger out gradually, pushing down towards the legs with the finger(s) while drawing the hand up towards the head.

Being postillioned is another way to open yourself up to new experiences. You may be nervous at first, from the newness of it; it may not seem pleasurable at all. Since your anus/rectum is used to nothing but excrement inside, a finger may cause you to feel like going to the bathroom. This is to be expected at first, and will disappear as you relax and get used to it. It's also easier if you're sexually excited. Keep in mind that the finger can't harm you unless it has a sharp nail or pokes violently.

Fist Fucking

In fist fucking the whole gloved hand (and even the forearm) goes up the rectum. Some people like this: they say it produces very erotic sensations of their internal organs. Although fist fucking can be very painful, it's not necessarily an S & M (sado-masochistic) action; any two people can get into it who want to. You can do fist fucking because the anus and rectum are so remarkably flexible. You start by bunching the fingertips together and inserting them, lubricated, in the anus. Then you slowly work the fingers up and in, as the anal sphincter relaxes. Finally, if the anus relaxes enough, you'll be able to fit the whole hand (with the fingertips still pressed together). Once in, you can clench the fist and slide your arm in too.

Of course, before you can be fist fucked, you must really want it and be able to relax your anus. Fist fucking can be very harmful if it bruises the prostate gland, causing infection, or irritates anal sores you already have, or pierces the rectum itself. If the rectum is broken, it's easy to get peritonitis, an infection inside the stomach cavity, which can be fatal without quick medical treatment. So, if you want to do fist fucking, be cautious.

△

The following alternative to fisting was written by W. L. Warner M.D. of the American Association of Physicians for Human Rights, and is reprinted, with permission, from *In the Heat of Passion: How to Have Safer, Hotter Sex* (Leyland Publications, 1987):

Fisting (or handballing in one vernacular) was one of the first sex practices identified as high risk for AIDS virus transmission, although the investigators failed to recognize the almost certain confounding element of the presence of semen in the rectums of those being fisted. Fisting with disposable gloves and without deposition of semen has been thought by some to be safe, since the AIDS virus would not be introduced. However, several investigators have now shown that the trauma, sometimes microscopic, to the rectum associated with stretching from the insertion of large objects may well lead to depression of the immune system of an HIV-positive "bottom" (fistee) from exposure of rectal contents to the blood stream. Such exposure may lead to "activation" of lymphocytes containing quiescent AIDS virus, resulting in replication and release of virus to invade more cells and converting a dormant disease state into an active one. *Such cautions apply to large dildos as well as the hand, of course.* The "top" (fister) is adequately protected by the glove. Thus the precaution applies to general health and well-being of the bottom rather than transmission of virus *per se.*

For the sexual satisfaction and enjoyment of ass-sensitive men (and most men are, even tops!), the substitution of "fingering" for fisting is recommended. Gentle prostatic massage with one or two fingers, sufficiently lubricated, can be a turn-on for most men without introducing trauma. The gloved finger is gently inserted to the point of feeling the heart-shaped organ (about the size of a small walnut); the crest or rounded portion is massaged from side to side while observing the bottom for specific movements which give optimal enjoyment. The top will be able to feel the tensing and enlargement of the gland if orgasm occurs, adding to his involvement in his partner's enjoyment. In the rare instance when gentle touching elicits pain, there is a medical question which needs to be evaluated; a prostatic infection may be the cause of the pain and massage should be discontinued.

Rimming

Rimming (also called "analingus") is another way to explore rear ends—it's licking, tonguing, and sucking the anus. This might seem like a strange thing to do, because asses are supposed to be dirty and bad. Actually, they're not. Although it's possible to catch V.D. or hepatitis from an infected person (see ch. 2), fears of rimming are mainly esthetic, that is, related to smell, taste, and personal preference. As with postillioning and anal intercourse, you can always douche beforehand, eliminating any odors and being of utmost cleanliness.

It's because the anus-opening is so delicately sensitive, and the lips and tongue so warmly expressive, that rimming is enjoyed by many people. It's also an easy thing to do, in any position where the buttocks can be drawn far enough apart to admit the tongue. Analingus is nice as part of *Around the World*, kissing and tonguing the body all over. You can lick across the anus in soft, wet strokes, or encircle it, going round and around languorously. You can flick the tongue-tip rapidly, or insert it inside as far as it'll go, pushing and stroking back and forth. You can brush the lips gently over the spot, or suck hard on the anus, as if trying to draw it out. This is specially nice if combined with tongue insertion. If, while you're being rimmed, you push down and relax the anus as if shitting, it will expand a little outwards, giving more area to caress and even nibble at.

It's also nice to combine analingus with scrotilingus, tonguing and sucking his balls. In fact, the whole area between the legs, since it's so protected, is soft and sensitive to touching and warmth.

△

Author's Note to new edition: Nowadays, due to the risk of HIV and hepatitis, only clearly-uninfected partners should engage in rimming, or some kind of barrier such as a latex dam should be used. Always assume your partner may be HIV-positive, unless you know conclusively otherwise. Read carefully the safe-sex guidelines on p. 37.

6

S & M
AND OTHER SCENES

The Orgy

Stephen and Michael were already naked on the floor, their genitals erect and trembling. When Sebastian arrived, Martin quickly released the prick from his pants and slipped it into his mouth. Bill entered Gerald from behind. Dennis, who was very attractive, found himself with a cock in his left hand, his right hand, in his mouth and in his anus. Peter, excited by the insistent presence of Walter's tongue in his asshole, came in Allen's face. Hibiscus and Tahara fell upon Scrumbly and Sepulchra. Surprisingly, they all came together. I myself made it with Christopher. I fondled the swollen organ out from his clothes and sucked it until the milk of his penis flowed in my throat. Many others were present. I've forgotten their names. Their pale bodies squirmed on the floor like libidinous trout in a shallow stream.

—James Mitchell

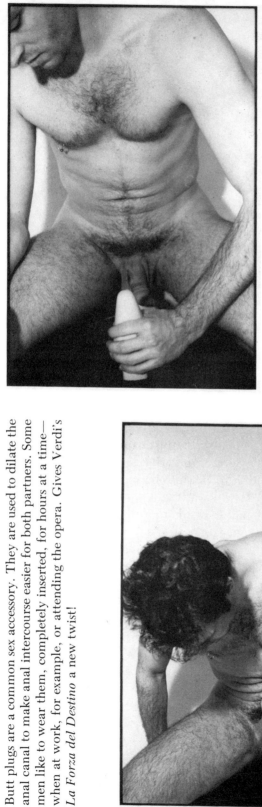

Butt plugs are a common sex accessory. They are used to dilate the anal canal to make anal intercourse easier for both partners. Some men like to wear them, completely inserted, for hours at a time—when at work, for example, or attending the opera. Gives Verdi's *La Forza del Destino* a new twist!

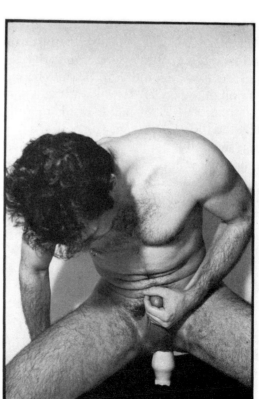

S & M
AND OTHER SCENES

So far in this book I've been talking about ways of sharing sex, about techniques—what you move, how you move it, and what to watch out for. And I've also been describing an emotional atmosphere, a context of trust, sharing, gentleness, honesty, and warmth. But there are some aspects of sex play which may be important to some people that I've left out of the discussion. One thing I've omitted is group sex, since I've only talked about you by yourself or with a partner. But one's or two's are not the only combinations.

I've also ignored sex roles—being dominant or submissive, playing master-and-slave, and so on. Many people get off on such roles and want to know more about them. Another thing for some is fetishes, objects of sex desire. And then there are also sex supplements, accessories like dildos and drugs to enhance your pleasure.

So for all of you who'd like to know more about these things, here are sections introducing "group sex," "S & M," "fetishes," "voyeurism," "sex accessories" and "drugs." These sections are not long and detailed, but short and suggestive, and certainly don't cover the full range of sex interests. They're meant to encourage further exploration if something interests you.

Group Sex

It may seem from previous chapters that *two* people is the only and ideal way to share sex and touching. But indeed, this would be a narrow way of looking at things; pairing is not the be-all and end-all of everything. It's only one out of many possibilities. Modern western culture romanticizes and idealizes the couple as the All-Enduring, Totally-Satisfying way to go. One keeps searching for that perfect mate, who'll supply everything.

This was not always the attitude of our society, nor of other societies. Pairing is a sexual pattern for reproducing the species, and is found in all genitally sexual animals. But animals usually change partners frequently, and in human cultures one relationship does not usually exclude others, nor is the pair the only style. Sometimes threesomes or group rituals of all different kinds are allowed or encouraged. Variety and flexibility are key themes in human behavior. There's certainly nothing wrong with pairing, as long as it doesn't become a delusional obsession.

I'd like to briefly look at sexual sharing between three and more men. This can involve discreet threesomes or hundred-person wild orgies.

Where gay sexuality has been allowed, such groupings have almost always happened. Reading through the historical sections of the past chapters, you'll note that sex in groups is often described, sometimes where everyone is sharing it, at other times where most are watching, or in which there's a group of pairs. For masturbation, fellatio, anal intercourse—all the ways—there are groups. In Chapter Three I reported ritual public masturbation in ancient Egypt and opium gatherings in China; in Chapter Four, there was the sex party in Malaya; in Chapter Five, ancient Celtic threesomes and puberty rites in New Guinea. These groups have a variety of purposes, religious communion, growth, and/or pleasure. In most cultures, including our own, sexual orgies have long been common. Many southern European artists have left us paintings of "daisy-chains," circles of men fucking, some of these depicting Egyptian or Turkish *es-silsileh* (circle).

Today there are few if any ritual ways for getting together in group sex. Private parties are one possibility. The private gay sex clubs in big cities are another (*provided one follows 100% safe-sex practices*). Many people like to share themselves with a group, and sensual/ sexual levels can certainly be a part of this.

What it takes is the desire to do it and the facilitation of group awareness towards this end. Any three or more people, under many circumstances, are potential material for group sex, if all want it and someone takes the initiative. When friends get together, they share information and entertainment. Why not sex as well?

In my work as a massage-group leader at gay raps, I've often seen group warmth and intimacy become sensual and sexual, and lead to marvelously supportive, growthful experiences. The major problem here is to avoid forcing anyone to participate; groups have the uncanny ability to demand conformity, to the degree that its members are scared of not doing what everybody else wants. So precaution must be taken against making group sex happen through force or fear. Other than this, it's undoubtedly a good thing, breaking through the social taboos against group warmth and touch. Again, talk will help in the matter: if it seems some people would like the idea, bring it up in the group as a possibility.

Usually some will begin touching and fondling. Once people get into it, it's best to be fairly loose about who does what, folks doing what they feel like; and remember, you *don't* have to participate. Mutual masturbation is probably the easiest sexual thing, hands going here and there. Or you can form a circle, doing yourself or your neighbor—this is called a "circle jerk." Others may want to get into fellatio or anal intercourse.

Fellatio is easy to do with three (and more). The classic style is for one person to lie on his back. Another, then, kneels over him, heads both pointing in the same direction. Then someone else can kneel over the first person's face or lie under the second person's legs. Such a chain can be extended to include however many people. Informally speaking, any way people want to lay/stand/kneel is fine, and lots of variety is possible.

For anal intercourse the kneeling position can be used, people on their knees or hands and knees, one behind the other—all insertors using condoms. Such chains are quite extravagant to watch or be in, but may be a little too formal for the typical orgy or menage à trois.

S & M

There are several ways to answer the question, what is S & M? We can say it's the acting out, during sex, of manipulation and/or punishment fantasies—that is, images or story-lines in your mind that turn you on, that excite you, and that involve things like torturing someone, or forcing them to do your will, or being tortured or forced to obey. From a practical point of view, S & M is the use of chains, handcuffs, leather thongs, belts, whips and other such items. It's also the playing of power roles, dominant/submissive, master/slave, disciplinarian, sadist/masochist. There are many different styles and varieties of S & M, but most of them involve someone being restrained (tied down and so on) and/or punished (whipped and so on) as part of the sexual sharing.

This doesn't mean that S & M is a brutal, one-sided activity, where the S (the sadist, the "dominant" partner in the scene) manipulates the *M* (the masochist, the "submissive" partner) against the M's wishes exclusively for the S's pleasure. On the contrary, S & M as usually practiced is entirely voluntary and of equal pleasure and sharing for both partners. In fact, it has to be entered into willfully, and enjoyed equally, by both, or no one has any fun.

This is what separates S & M sex from the popular images of "sadists" and "masochists." In the social myth a sadist is an evil, fiendish creature out to inflict horrible cruelties, tortures, and mutilation on innocent victims, as with "the sadists at Auschwitz" and "the sadistic rapist." Masochists, on the other hand, are popularly thought of as pathetic, wretched, will-less wrecks who grovel and beg for humiliation and punishment. But neither of these images applies to S & M sex. In fact, both of them are actually expressions of social condemnation of S & M, in the same way that the "faggot" image is a put-down of gay men. Such stereotypes are meant to keep people away from these interests by frightening them.

Because of this, there are a lot of people with S & M interests who deny their desires since they're afraid of doing something "bad," of turning into a horrible monster. But I'd say that S & M sex fantasies, of controlling or being controlled, of punishing or being punished, are fairly common.

I don't think it's easy to face and accept S & M desires if you've been taught to fear and deny them. If you have them, such desires are an important part of you, and can teach you a lot about yourself and relating to others. But it's easy to feel threatened by them, that you'll wind up doing terrible things, or that you'll become some kind of creepy, slimy creature of the night. And there is a small chance of something like this happening if you can't maintain your sense of integrity and self-respect. So I don't think you should force yourself to get into S & M fantasies against your sense of caution.

As with all parts of yourself, you can simply start out by just paying attention, being aware of positive S & M feelings inside. Be gentle with them; don't push them and don't let them push you. At first, they're like strange, shy creatures hiding in trees and under rocks. You're curious, so you sit and watch and see if one will come out, but you don't try to get too close since you don't know if they'll hurt you or not. There's no need to rush things; take as long as you want.

After paying attention for a while, you'll begin to see your fantasies more clearly, and they won't seem as scary as they used to. Get to know your S & M desires, and you'll begin to accept them. And you'll discover that as you accept them as a part of yourself, you'll still be OK, you won't turn into some kind of ogre. You'll find that being bound and punished, or binding and punishing, are enjoyable parts of you, worthy of respect and appreciation.

By a gradual, growing process you can come together with your S & M desires and explore them in your mind. You might talk to someone about them, to help clarify your explorations. Then at some point you may want to try acting them out and see what happens.

There are at least several established S & M subcultures in any large gay community. When most people think of S & M sex, they usually think of the well-defined, more-or-less formal activities of these subcultures. And one of the best ways to learn about S & M is to join in the scene. But S & M interests don't have to be so formal, and you don't have to learn all about the scenes, roles and equipment to enjoy them.

S & M can be nothing more than a wrestling match in bed, or squirming and pushing, pinching and biting as you get aroused with your partner. If you want to go farther, it's easy to get more into your S & M fantasies with him, if both of you want to. The first step is to tell him about your fantasies and to hear about his. Maybe you and/or he would like to be spanked with a belt. Another simple thing to do is tie your partner down on the bed with ropes or straps and slowly jack him off—the delights can be ecstatic. If you try this, make sure the bonds aren't too tight (since the idea is to restrain him, not hurt or cut off the circulation), and be ready to release him after it's over so he doesn't get muscle spasms.

When getting into these things, it's always important to let your partner know what's happening, and to be clear to him about what you want and what's going to happen. That way you'll be able to find out what you like without hurting anyone or getting hurt, and without turning anyone off. In S & M sex, both partners always give their willing consent, and no one *ever* has to participate without wanting to, without pleasure.

It may be unclear at first what kinds of S & M you enjoy, and how far you'd like to get into it. If you don't want to act out your fantasies at all, That's fine, but if you do, there's a lot to get into. First of all, there are the two roles, S and M. Then, there are different fantasies, of bondage, punishment, and humiliation. And then, there are also differing styles of dress and equipment—leather and rubber, for example. These are all aspects of the S & M scene, and to know if they're for you, you have to try them out. Not everybody does everything; most people have definite tastes.

The way to get started is to meet some people. You can do this by two routes: answering ads or going to certain bars. Some gay publications, such as *Bay Area Reporter* or *Drummer*, carry S & M ads. These are usually specific and will give you an idea of what you might be getting into. Then you can answer one you like and explain what your interests/ experiences are. [See also the several mail-order S & M books on p. 160.]

On the other hand, in most large cities there are certain bars (and sometimes bath-houses also) known to attract an S & M crowd. Such bars are usually cowboy and/or leather places. That is, when you go in a leather bar, for example, you discover a lot of men wearing heavy boots, jackets, vests, pants, hats and sometimes studded collars and chains—all

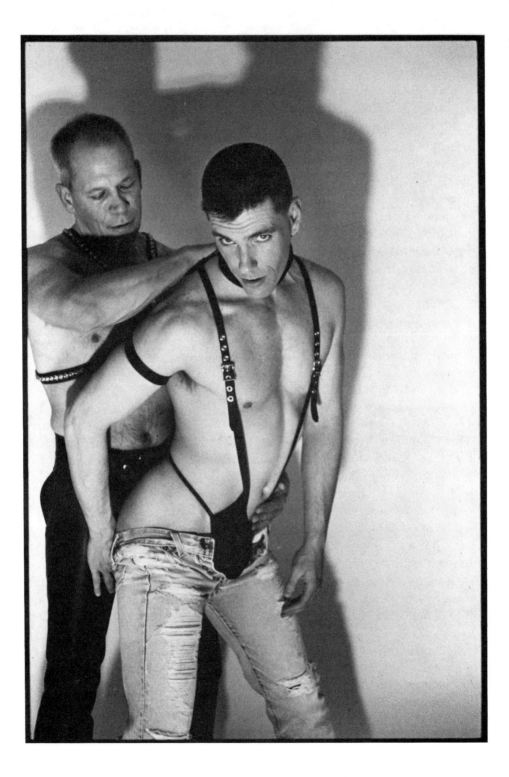

usually in black leather (or denim). Not all people wearing leather will be into S & M, and vice versa. But there will be many who do.

Without going into these costume scenes in detail, let's just say that the get-up (or *kit* as it's called) is for making an impression, creating an effect—you pretend to be who you want by dressing up that way. As a wild biker, as a hot, commanding cowboy. It doesn't matter who you are outside, at work or on Sundays; all that's important is your image at the moment, your ideal. It's a form of dressing up, of play-acting. Since the costume crowds are rather clannish against outsiders, you must be willing to accept their dress code to get in. So, when you go to one of these places to meet someone it's best to dress a little like they do (don't overdo it, though, when you don't know what you're doing yet).

Next is meeting someone. Here a lot depends on what role you want to take, that of the S or the M. S & M writers advise the novice to always take the M role, even if they feel like being an S, because they won't know what to do at first, and it takes experience and confidence to be a good S. Also, these same writers say that to be a good S, you must know what it's like to be the M and that takes experience in the role. Although most people wind up being mainly an S or an M, many enjoy and do both.

Often the newcomer wants to take the S role thinking it's more "appropriate" or "masculine," but this is surprisingly untrue. Both roles are equally "appropriate" and "masculine" within the S & M context, and on a deeper level, both involve equal amounts of participation and control. Often, in fact, it's the M in control, who gets the S to set up and act out the M's particular fantasies.

Getting back to the bar, once you have this in mind you then go about finding someone who'll take you home and teach you a few things. They say you can tell an S by a set of keys, chains, gloves or an earring on the left side of the body, while the M has his on the right. But this is not always true. You have to talk it over with him to find out if he interests you. Be honest, and tell him you're just starting out and what you want to get into. Also, as you're talking to him you must decide whether you can trust him or not. A sense of basic trust is primary for a good S & M experience, so don't go home with him unless you feel he's OK.

Once you're home there are many things he can do with you. But before you start it's essential that you agree on an out-signal, a word or sign that lets him know you've had enough and are freaking out, so he'll stop. Otherwise, he may just keep going.

Depending on your mutual interests, several kinds of action can then happen. One of these is *restraints*, objects used to limit the freedom of the body. These include handcuffs, gags, leg-irons, straps, ropes, chains, tying posts, racks and so on. One common object is a cock-ring, a small ring of leather or metal which goes around the base of the penis or around the penis and testicles, and which can help keep the penis stiff, or make it larger, or distend the balls (make them stick out from the body), or for attaching straps or weights. And again, contrary to the popular stereotype, restraints aren't usually meant to cause pain or discomfort, but to enclose and limit the body. For many, pain very often detracts from the fun of restraints.

Then there's *punishment*, most typically some kind of striking with the hand, a paddle, a strap, a whip, a cat-o-nine-tails and so on. Probably the simplest object is an ordinary leather belt, which, when doubled over, makes a smart sting and loud whack without being too painful. The idea is to give a pleasurable irritation, to heighten excitement and sensation.

Again, keep in mind that these people are doing all this because they're getting off on it. Some critics think S & M is bizarre and perverted, but I don't think so—perversion is in the eye of the beholder. Maybe "normal" sex is just the timid expression of shallow, frightened, polite desire. Is "pain" and "suffering" always painful, always dark and bad? In some cases, the M is enjoying the pain itself, while in others he's heightening his pleasure through the pain, like biting and straining during an ordinary orgasm.

There's also *humiliation*, belittling the M, which is part of bondage and punishment, but can extend to things like bootlicking, grovelling and watersports, that is, pissing on the M. This is part of a "heavier" S & M scene which you can discover as you gain experience.

Some people will be into all these things while others will only be into some. Also, they can be done anywhere from lightly to heavily or intensely. That is, you can use mild restraints like handcuffs only, all the way up to complex harness/strap/pulley combinations for lifting a heavily weighted and bound M off the floor. In the same way, you can have no pain involved, which is what many people prefer, or intense pain, which is the special delight of some.

Although it may seem like all these S & M activities are done chaotically, there's actually a set of rules and structure that goes with them. These rules are meant to guide two (or more) people into sharing and enjoying deep, powerful desires and needs, while making sure things happen mutually, that no one is taken advantage of. The structure involves such things as establishing trust and rapport, and setting limits. These rules of the S & M game are good to know about, and you'll discover them as you meet experienced people. Most S & M folks will be happy to share their knowledge with willing, cooperative beginners.

Often being restrained gives a sense of freedom, since then you can express yourself, thrash about, cry and so on, knowing that it's OK and to be expected. The S and M roles allow some people to do things they want but ordinarily can't. S & M may help some to express their totality, by exposing deeper yearnings and underlying personality. The S only need be an S during the sex play, and so too for the M. At work or with family they might be entirely different people. S & M may allow them to act out desires which otherwise could build into frustrations or get acted out under inappropriate situations, for example at work or on the street.

However, some gay people have criticized S & M as a way of maintaining narrow consciousness and oppressive sex-role values. As one critic says, "For gay males, the appeal [of S & M] is to be part of the American *Man's* fantasy of omnipotence, control, domination. Its symbology is not of cooperation, but one of conflict, ordering and serving." Critics point out that many S & M spokespeople and practitioners are politically and culturally conservative. There is controversy about the consciousness-raising potential of S & M; some people feel that it inhibits personal and political change. I think these arguments point out that S & M contains both constructive and destructive potentials, and that it's important to be aware of both sides.

Through your explorations into S & M you may discover a lasting interest or a passing phase. Keep in mind that if you're interested in growing, growth is always a process, and never a thing or a goal. All roles are things, the acting out of conscious or unconscious patterns, and if you play roles to discover their roots and become your wholeness, your center, you will be growing. But if you merely act out roles unconsciously they will manipulate you and block your growth.

Perhaps the essence of S & M is controlled violence. Every human has violence, has a whole secret side in the mind full of chaotic animal passions like hatred, lust, ruthlessness and terror, and desires for power, to manipulate, dominate and submit. In order to become a complete human being, every person must explore this side of themselves and learn to accept it. If you are aware of this, the feelings experienced in S & M can be a gateway to this dark side, opening the hidden negative forces to the light of consciousness.

If you only see your S & M activities as times of pleasurable humiliation, hatred, manipulation, suffering and so on, S & M can just as well form the block beyond which insight never goes. Then the fantasies are controlling you, and make it very hard for you to see these chaotic forces as the other side of your "normal" daytime self. It's easy to just play them out over and over again like an endless record and miss the chance of exploring the unity of your dark and light aspects in a centered wholeness.

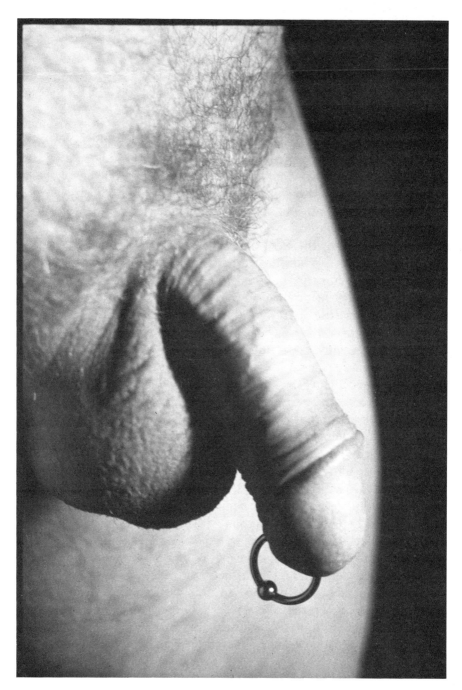

Cock piercing with the Prince Albert ring (named after Queen Victoria's Germanic consort) has become a popular sex fashion in the 1990s. The piercing heightens sensuality for both wearer and partner. In anal intercourse an extra strong latex condom with extra space at the end (such as Pleasure Plus brand) should be used, or double bagging. Several methods of piercing are used, and these should be done only by a professional (such as those of *Gauntlet*—with shops in San Francisco, Los Angeles & New York). Professionals suggest being fitted with the smallest size ring which is comfortable when the cock is erect.

Fetishes

A fetish is an object that turns you on sexually, that possesses an alluring, exciting mystique or power. All kinds of different things can become fetishes for people, and most have experienced at least some interest in a fetish. For many men with gay sex interests, for example, the erect penis is a fetish: they're mysteriously, uncontrollably drawn, it intoxicates them, they worship it. The penis becomes a power irrespective of its owner, an independent spirit and pleasure source. This has historical precedents: in many ancient societies, the phallus was quite literally worshipped as a god. Sometimes the person under the spell of a fetish doesn't recognize that this is the case, but is controlled by it none the less.

Of course, there's nothing particularly "wrong" or "bad" in having fetishes. On the contrary, they can enhance your experience. For example quite often in a leather scene it's a special piece of clothing or equipment that stimulates intense desire. For many it's the leather itself, its smell and touch, which drives them wild. For other people, rubber clothes and objects are especially appealing—in fact, there's a whole rubber scene devoted to such fetishes. I myself sometimes have a weakness for jockey shorts, although I can't explain it or account for it.

In some cases the person won't get excited without the fetish. Some leather people admit that it's the leather, and the scene just isn't the same without it. Occasionally a person is excited by their fetish alone, and everything else is insignificant. These are the kind of people called "fetishists" in the social mythology, and they're usually portrayed as bizarre perverts. A typical image is the middle-aged man who begs women for their shoes, or steals their underwear to sneak home and get off on his booty. But again, I don't think there's anything wrong with being a fetishist as long as you can get satisfaction without forcing anyone against their will.

Boots, gloves, scarves, and various body limbs are common fetishes. For a while we were reading in the newpapers about a "foot rapist," who would sneak up on people and force them to bare a foot, which the "rapist" would then caress before fleeing. Other things that may become fetishes include bottles of perfume, eye glasses, dirty socks, and even motorcycles. For some an object touched or worn by a beloved person takes on fetishistic qualities.

Getting in touch with fetish-interests is a good idea, if you think you might have some. You can explore them with yourself and others, and make rituals around them, such as special prayers and acts of respect. This can help you touch the mythic/mystic side of your being, if you do it with awareness and a recognition of what you are about.

Genderfuck

One of the things that always scared me the most about the gay world was transvestites. At first they just bothered me a lot, and I thought such people were very sick. But then I came to realize that what was bothering me wasn't the transvestites at all, but some kind of fear about myself. After paying a lot of attention to this, I began to see that I was afraid of my own womanhood, but secretly attracted to it. Over a period of time I gathered up enough courage, and finally plunged into cross dressing myself.

I did this in a way called *genderfuck*. Genderfuck is dressing like a man and a woman at the same time, in an exaggerated, colorful way. It's wearing dresses, jewelry and pastel makeup with glitter in your beard. You can do it just a little, say, putting on eyeshadow, or go all the way with a full costume including shoes and hat. Properly speaking, genderfuck is different from transvestism. In transvestism, someone dresses up to impersonate, to imitate a member of the other sex. In genderfuck, you have fun being all the sexes at once. Both styles can be very pleasurable and also politically meaningful.

I really enjoyed doing genderfuck, going to parties and bars with purple eyeshadow and baggy pink satin pants. The fun, the playfulness of it, helped me break through my fears. I discovered what my "feminine" qualities were, that I liked these qualities, and that they gave me strength. In other words, a whole new side of myself was opened up: being intuitively powerful, darkly moist, yielding, empathic, transcendental, like the ocean and the mountains. Further, genderfuck helped teach me to see that sex roles, being a "man" or a "woman," are just as much fantasies external to my true nature as any other kind of play-role.

Voyeurism

Another common sex interest is voyeurism, which is enjoyment through watching other people have sex. You can do this either openly or secretly, with or without their consent. I admit to voyeuristic tendencies, and I remember times of secretly watching others. I have often felt guilty about these times, because it seemed the wrong thing to do.

But it surely can be enjoyable. Some people like to specialize in voyeurism, either overt or covert. It's often easy to make arrangements with friends, or at a party, to join in their sex-play by watching, and many people are excited by the thought of having someone watch. You can also

A dildo is a popular, generally safe sex toy (but see also *caveat* on p. 114). Try always to use your own personal dildo and wash well after use. Avoid dildos with wires in them. In this photo the model's own dildo (center) is flanked by the super-cocks (in dildo form) of Jeff Stryker (on left) and Chris Lord (on right). Cock pumps are another fun sex toy and can be used with partners to make your cocks thicker. Directions should be followed carefully.

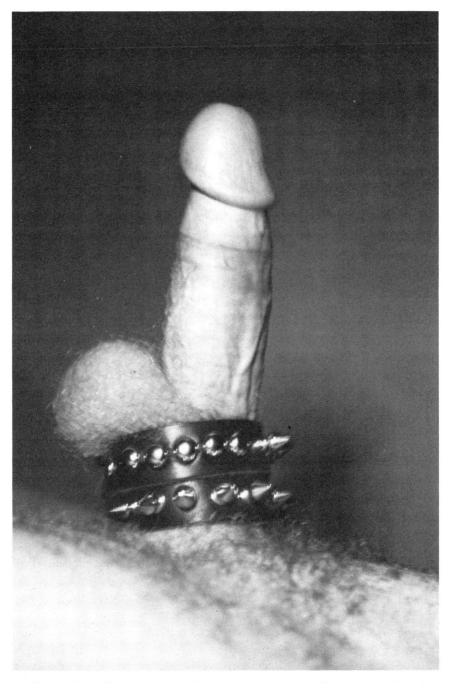

Cock rings have become a popular sex accessory over the past two decades. They come in different designs and can be bought in sex shops or through the mail (see ads in gay publications). They encircle the balls and the base of the cock and keep the cock engorged and hard for longer lasting sex.

watch sex play on videos, now easily purchased via mail. I think it's probably better if you can be open about voyeurism, because doing it on the sly is so easily guilt-provoking. One simple voyeuristic thing is to have someone masturbate himself for you. There are lots of other things, which I'm sure you can think up with a little imagination.

Sex Accessories

Sex aids are things to make your sexual experience easier or more intense. Such aids are very common, and most people have used at least one on occasion. Throughout this book I've referred to an important sex aid, lubricants. A lubricant is usually necessary for anal intercourse, and also good for masturbation and body rubbing. *Only* a water-based lubricant (such as KY) should be used with condoms. Other lubricants (scented or flavored oils) can be used for massage. It's important, too, not to put anything with soap up the rectum, as this upsets the rectal eco-system.

Besides lubricants, there's a wide range of stimulating aids to enhance your pleasure. Such as dildos, for example. A dildo is a long, firm object, other than a penis or fingers, inserted up the ass. This can feel very nice, due to the sensexual nature of the anus, rectum and prostate gland. A dildo can be helpful when you're by yourself or with a friend, where it provides extra excitement during fellatio, masturbation and so on. Many couples get quite a kick out of dildos during their sexual sharing.

Dildos can be bought in most adult book stores/sex shops. They're usually made of rubber or plastic and come in different shapes and sizes. Some come equipped with soft, quill-lined sides (called "French sleeves"), or with vibrators, or hoses for enema-like injections. In a pinch you can use a cucumber, but I do not recommend candles, bottles, or broom handles because they can break in half, shatter, or splinter, respectively. It's quite possible to lose objects in the rectum and then be unable to get them out without a doctor. Of course, when you use a dildo lubricate it first.

Other sex aids include: the P.A.S. (Penis Aid Stimulator), a hollow dildo which fits over the penis to make it bigger, for use during anal intercourse; sets of metal or plastic balls on a string, which, when inserted up the rectum, can be pulled out at orgasm for extra thrills; various vibrators, electric masturbators, tubes and sleeves to put against or over the penis for jacking off; and so on. All these aids can be found at the well-supplied sex shop, as can the various leather/chain objects, such as cockrings, straps, and harnesses, mentioned in the S & M section.

Drugs

There are also various drugs which may enhance your sexual pleasure. The best known are alcohol and marijuana/hashish, although these are not, strictly speaking, aphrodisiacs. What booze does is fuzz up the mind, so that you tend to forget anxieties, social rules, shyness, and personality hangups. A lot of liquor tends to inhibit erections.

Marijuana (and hashish, which is the dried oil from marijuana) is a mild mind enhancer, which relaxes the body and increases body sensitivity. Because of this, touch and pleasure feelings become stronger and more colorful. Also controls fall slack, as with alcohol. Many people enjoy marijuana to enhance their pleasures.

Then there's amyl nitrate, commonly known as "poppers." This is inhaled through the nose, and causes the blood vessels to the heart to dilate, bringing on a euphoric "rush" lasting several minutes. Some people sniff poppers during sex and especially at orgasm to multiply their sensations. However, the drug has a very bad effect on weak hearts, and can kill in some cases. So don't use it unless your heart's in good condition.

Other drugs, such as valiums, LSD ("acid"), heroin ("junk"), cocaine ("coke"), amphetamines ("uppers" like "speed" and "whites"), barbiturates ("downers" like "reds" and "bennies"), and so on, are not usually related to sexual activity. Some, like the barbiturates, even suppress it, while others, like valiums, inhibit erection. The exception to this is quaaludes, a kind of relaxant, which seems to eliminate many barriers to sex, although it too reduces erection firmness. However, quaaludes are physically addicting and have been, for the most part, removed from drug markets.

In relation to S & M sex, most of these drugs distract from the action and can be positively dangerous! If you're thinking of getting into an S & M scene, beware of going along with anyone who is very drunk or stoned, or who plans to get this way while binding you up or beating you. It's no fun to be trapped with someone who's been carried away or freaked out on some kind of drug. For this reason, almost all regular S & M people avoid drug-taking, except for a little alcohol or marijuana at first to loosen things up. Occasionally, poppers are also used for an extra flash. Sometimes, you'll run across someone who needs a certain amount of some drug like booze to remove their inhibitions, who'll be timid or dull beforehand but an excited participant when a little (or very) tipsy. In general, it's best to exercise caution in such situations.

7

LOVE AND GAY CONSCIOUSNESS

Come I will make the continent indissoluble,
I will make the most splendid race the sun ever shone upon,
I will make divine magnetic lands,
With the love of comrades,
    With the life-long love of comrades.

*   *   *

We two, how long we were fool'd,
Now transmuted, we swiftly escape as Nature escapes,
We are nature, long have we been absent, but now we return . . .
We have circled and circled till we have arrived home again, we two,
We have voided all but freedom and all but our own joy.

—Walt Whitman, *Leaves of Grass*

LOVE AND GAY CONSCIOUSNESS

It might seem from the chapters of this book, that the world is made of sex, that a hard cock is the greatest thing in the world, and that sex is the most desirable and fantastic human joy. It might also seem like I believe there's only one way of having sex, and only one purpose to it, ejaculation. But I hope you don't get these impressions. All I've tried to do is describe *how* you can have sex by yourself and with others if you want to. Sex is just another way of being and doing. A lot of information has been hidden from us, and there's a need for clear, simple explanation. This I've tried to do here, because I've known too many men who got hurt, because they just didn't know the precautions to take in sucking and ass-fucking. I've known too many men who didn't even believe it was OK to fondle another man.

There are many people who've been hurt by the anti-gayness of our society, who feel pain and fear along with their gay desires. Sex. Touch. Care. Love. What are these to me? I want them, I need them, I *need* to hold a man (a male human) in my arms, to be warm and loving with him. But another part of me says, "That's bad, that's wrong, ugly, dirty—you're a pervert, a faggot!" There were times when I felt like killing myself, it got so bad.

Denying bad feelings—pretending they don't exist—won't make them go away. They just go underground and cause trouble. Only becoming aware of them—accepting them as your feelings—will work, for then they become a part of your wholeness and melt into your strength and beauty. Many of us with gayness have had to suffer a great deal, and it's only natural to try to escape from pain. But even though there may be a lot of it deep down from years of hiding and pretending, touching a little of this badness at a time will slowly clear it up, clean it out and allow our greater selves to unfold.

I'm not supposing here that you have problems (I don't know if you do or not), or that gay people are sick, or that you should get into suffering, or go see a psychiatrist. Rather, I'm only suggesting you pay attention to all of you, and if you find feelings inside that're frightening, I want you to know that you don't have to hide from them, and hide them from others. There are other people with gay feelings, who know what it means to be confused, and if you're in need of support or help, they're there to help out. In many cities now, there are openly gay counselors, therapists, and community friends. We help each other, by being honest and supportive. Reaching-out has taught me the value of honest giving and receiving, and being more real.

Being Yourself

Another of my fears in writing this book has been that sex techniques will be seen as a way to escape problems, that people will say, "If only I was more skillful, more clever at sucking cock, if only I could really abandon myself to ecstatic sex and give my friend the perfect orgasm—if only I could do all this—I'd be a more pleasant, enjoyable, successful, loveable, loving, loved, happy, sweet, and carefree person." As with any pleasurable interest, sex can become an escape from the troubles and pains of life, a way to "prove" yourself and gain *meaning* in a dirty, cold world. This escapist attitude leads to an emphasis on *performing*, on comparing yourself with a machine, being efficient: "Was I good enough?" This also leads to becoming an *object* to be bought and sold: "I'm horny, so I'll dress up perfectly, and go sell myself at the bar." It's easy to make a plastic game out of love: everyone would rather have a new Cadillac than an old Volkswagen. Be cute, be hot, be a winner.

Sex guides in general have played up to people's fears of being lonely, inadequate and insecure, about being good or loveable, by turning people into sex machines—the more sophisticated and effective you are in bed, the more worthwile you must be. Be agreeable, go along with everything, don't be a bore. Don't be a loser.

So I say that sex techniques aren't important. All these things I've written about—motions, positions, skills—are not worth much at all. The skills of sex are like the skills of rope climbing—the more you know, the better it gets done. But sex is not usually something to get done, to get it over with. In fact, I don't think sex is often done for just its own sake. For sure, it's true that if you're hungry, you want to eat, and if you're horny, you want to come. But being physically intimate automatically has so many meanings, that just using someone to climax must mean ignoring all these

140

other things—touch, care, warmth, your needs, his needs. And these needs will not be met unless you're aware of them and respond to them.

So, sucking cock good will not make you happy. It may give you some pleasure and satisfaction, but only for a short while. What is happiness, you ask? Ah, only you can answer that. And here is the topic of this last chapter: you, who you are, and what your potential is as a human being. Our culture is constantly trying to tell us who we should be, and how we should go about living. Since sex is a big part of life, it becomes connected with a whole lot of "shoulds," do this, don't do that, be programmed like a robot. For me, all these "shoulds" are chains on my freedom.

So because this is a consciousness book, it's about more than sex. It's about touching, and the spirit of touching. *What is spirit?* Let me answer that by asking you a question, *who are you?* What do you want in life? What do you want to be?

If I had been writing this book several years ago, I'd have praised sex gloriously, and ignored all this other stuff. But I've found too little in *just sex* for me. I want more.

Each of you will have to consider all this for yourself. I don't want you to think I'm down on casual sex or safe-sex promiscuity. Far from it! Being spontaneous, just following sudden whims and urges is great adventure. I hope in this book I've suggested a few more ways to go about getting what you want. But just as I wanted to point out that you can gag on a penis, or tear someone's rectum, so too you can burn a sensitive feeling. So I say, if you don't want to climax, if you don't want a hard on, this is just as good as wanting them. It's just as enjoyable and noble to cuddle as to fuck. If your penis goes soft, or doesn't even get hard, it does *not* mean you have failed. Maybe, in fact, your being soft is a great success, a victory for care over performance.

Warm bodies are spiritual. Even a ten-minute quickie in the bathroom with some stranger, involves touching. I want to encourage the spirit of touching, the warmth of bodies. I want to break down all the rules about touching, the taboos and fears of warmth. This is no easy thing to do, and here I just want to bring your attention to it. I'm sure I have as many hangups and confusions about touching as you do. But I can't help looking forward to the day when people stop playing all our silly games and move on to better things.

And the games I mean are those of alienation and pain, that encourage distance, suspicion and confusion in oneself and between people, that discourage growth, love, and care. Games like power, money, sexism, stereotyping and competition. But then, on the other hand, there are many games that are good for growth, that can open new doors.

Fantasies

In general, games both healthy and harmful are connected to fantasies, and it is your fantasies that have great power in shaping who you are and how to live, sexually, sensually and spiritually.

What are fantasies? They're imaginative pictures and thoughts in your mind that turn you on, that make you excited or fearful or loving or yearning. Often we don't notice our fantasies because they happen so quickly and easily, in a hazy, vague sort of way. This is because they come from the unconscious.

There are many kinds of fantasies. Some are images: your perfect lover, how you see yourself ideally, the body type that excites you. Others are stories: you conquer the world like Alexander; a beautiful stranger comes and takes you away with him; something bad will happen to you tomorrow. Such fantasies affect us constantly; often we'll imagine them in something or someone else. Then they're called projections, for example when I walk into a bar and there's my perfect lover standing at the counter—I *project* my fantasy onto him.

To get more in touch with your fantasies you have to pay attention to them. As you go about your daily life, try to notice your mental images and the emotion-packed ways you experience other people. A good thing to do is pay attention to strangers you pass on the street—how do they affect you? Are they scary, pitiful, intriguing, beautiful? Who turns you on and how? What would you like to do with that person? Follow your fancy where it will and see what turns up, what kind of story you can imagine; this is called daydreaming.

Many of your fantasies may seem "wrong" or may frighten you. But don't let that scare you off. Try to be impartial and observe them as if you were someone else. This can only help your self-understanding and growth.

For example, I sometimes have a very enjoyable fantasy of torturing beautiful nude men on a medieval rack. This used to frighten me a lot because I thought I must be a very bad person to have such an idea and enjoy it. I was afraid that one day I might try to act on it and cause a lot of trouble. But as I paid more attention to this fantasy, as if it was a curious story that I happened to enjoy, it gradually lost much of its frightening aspect and I saw that I didn't have to be a bad person for it. That I could respect my fantasy, appreciate it, and still control it. As it turns out, everyone has fantasies that seem horrible and fearsome to them, and in all cases these fantasies can be accepted and often acted on in some way. If, however, you feel like a fantasy is going to freak you out or take control of you, the best thing you can do is talk about it with someone you respect.

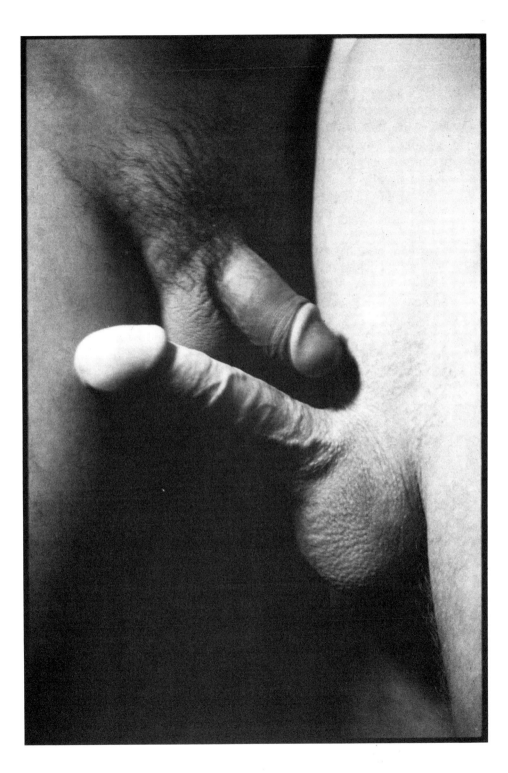

One of the best ways to learn about your fantasies is to do them consciously, to act them out in an aware way. Often this means playing a role, becoming a tough leather Angel, or queen of the ball. To me all roles are fantasies, and if you discover and play a new role for yourself, with full awareness of what you are doing, you can't help but learn more about who you really are, and through this grow in freedom.

Let your fantasies flow and they will enhance your experience. If you like, tell him about them and hear about his also. Try acting them out with him (if you already haven't), after getting his consent first, of course. This may draw you to playing roles like sadist and masochist, or using foods, scents, or mechanical aids, or wearing special clothes or costumes. Get dressed up, play-act, free your imagination. Feel your deeper desires and most fragile yearnings.

For many people, important fantasies relate to their childhood and their family. Fantasies of being your mother or your father, or needing them for support, or taking revenge on them, or abandoning them or being abandoned. These deeper fantasies may seem confusing, and you may feel sensitive or uncomfortable about them. But if they're there, it's certainly good to know what's going on. Often such fantasies control people in harmful ways, and yet are hard to recognize. One way to find them is to look for repeating patterns in your life that cause you unhappiness, such as always having the same kind of breakups with your lovers, or always failing at certain tasks. It's easy to get lost in such fantasies, and at some point you may want to visit a counselor or therapist who can help untangle them.

By getting in touch with your fantasies you can discover a lot about yourself. You can unlock the whole realm of creative imagination, which is the source of intuition and wisdom, of dreams and hopes, beauty and wonder. You can free yourself into emotional and instinctual urges—anger, lust, hatred, vengeance, terror, yearning—and find safely expressive ways. You can learn about power relations, how people oppress and manipulate themselves and each other. But for all this to happen, you must do it with self-awareness, with conscious recognition of what you are about, and why you are doing it. Consciousness makes all the difference—with it, you can grow, without it, you will become trapped in the powers of your unconscious and the ruts of mindless habit.

Fantasies are two-edged, with potential for good or bad karma to yourself and the world. Your unconscious is like a whole separate world of power, of images and landmarks. If you aren't careful, it can seduce you and trap you. But if you remember who you are, and look for your center, you can tap your hidden energies and beauty.

By playing fantasies and acting out roles, I discovered that I am weak as well as strong, passive as well as active, intuitive as well as rational. I discovered my wholeness, and I enjoy it. I found I like being vulnerable, sometimes out of control; that I like being spontaneous and honest, and angry when I feel it. And I especially like being nurturant—giving warmth, protection, love, life to others, being kind, gentle. Sometimes I know what to do, and sometimes I don't. I give, I take, I'm soft and hard and resourceful and foolish and wise. I become much more than I thought.

There are various levels of fantasy, of unconscious forces. These can be followed deeper and deeper inside, leading to extraordinary places and

experiences. These meta-normal places can be shared with another just as well as those I've already mentioned. For example, did you know that there's an eastern spiritual method of love, called tantric sex, in which the lovers try to become gods in sexual ecstasy? This is a remarkable fantasy indeed, and besides, it works! Tantra was developed for male/female couples, but I think it can be just as good for gay lovers. If you're intrested in this, I suggest you read up on it—one good, simple book I've found is Moffett's *Tantric Sex* (Berkley: N.Y., 1974).

Mystical Aspects of Gay Love

There's another mystical aspect of being with a man. This has to do with magic, with fantastic powers beyond our ordinary daily living. We easily get caught up in the mundane aspects of life. We go to work, we shop in the market for our food, we do the plain ordinary ho-hum things like eating, breathing, walking and sleeping. Because the plodding activities of daily life are pretty boring, it's easy for the whole world to seem dull, shallow and necessary.

But there's a whole other level of reality around us, entirely different in form and essence. This reality is extra-mundane and super-ordinary, but our modern life puts it down, so it gets to seem strange and foreign. In ancient days, and in many other cultures, this reality was given great respect and due, and known as God and Tao and the Great Mother, and wood nymphs, animal spirits, tree demons and devils. There were prayers and rituals and initiations—whole cultures revolved around the meanings and practices of religions, cults, mysteries and superstitions.

But too often today we think all that was primitive and immature, just crazy fantasies and beneath us. The thing is, though, that it's still here, inside us, and we continue to experience this other reality, except that we're not so aware of it, and often don't recognize it.

Probably one of the most common ways we get in touch with a spiritual force is through a lover. I think we tend to take love and sexual fantasies for granted, as things that just happen, but it's good to look down to the root-source of these things and find the powers lurking there. When we fall in love with someone something special happens—we're transported to euphoric highs and the most common things start glowing with warm light. The beloved takes on a special *power* and *wonder* and *meaning*.

What's the nature of this love, and why does it seem so wonderful? I think it's because it unlocks the secret reality, the secret self inside each of us, and provides a doorway to revelations and growth and true human maturity. When we fall in love with another man, we're getting in touch with an unconscious spirit-source, by evoking it in our beloved. We can follow this magic back inside us to its source, and use it to uncover our real nature. For it turns out that we're not just the mundane pedal-pushers we've been taught to believe. Far from it!

It's hard to talk about the unconscious spirit-forces because they're so different from the mundane daytime world most of us live in. In the past they took the form of powerful gods and fetish-statues to be worshipped. Today they sometimes take the form of a lover who seems so wonderful that we want to worship him. So we tend to see and experience these forces as personifications, as persons, even though they're more like vague cosmic cloud-themes living at a very deep, remote place in each of us. Keeping this in mind, I'd like to describe how I see these forces in love, and talk about some of the ways they manifest in life and art.

The secret gay love-source in the mind I call *the Double*. The Double may manifest in several forms, such as the Partner and the Puer Eternus. For a man, *the Partner* is the eternal image, inside him, of himself as beautiful, strong, in the form of a companion, a twin, a helping brother of magic power and sweetness. In "The Secret Sharer" by Joseph Conrad a man is confronted by his Partner: "it was, in the night, as though I had been faced by my own reflection in the depth of a sombre and immense mirror." The partner is often portrayed in old myths, such as *The Epic of Gilgamesh*, where a graceful, virtuous hero named Enkidu comes to help Gilgamesh and be his lover. In the *Iliad*, the Partner appears as the beloved friend of Achilles, Patroklos, who causes the hero to fulfill his fate. And in the Bible, he's the youth who saves David from the wrathful Saul and aids him, of whom David said, "my brother Jonathan: very pleasant hast thou been unto me: thy love to me was wonderful, passing the love of woman."

Because the Partner is one's deeper spirit-self and support, when two lovers evoke it between them they can gain strength and power. That's why many ancient armies, such as the Spartan and the Theban Sacred Band, encouraged soldier-lovers. This also happened among the Samurai in Japan. I believe this spirit-essence exists in each of us, and can be tapped for our own growth and joy. As Confucius wrote, commenting on fellowship, in the *I Ching*,

> But when two people are at one in their innermost hearts,
> They shatter even the strength of iron or bronze.
> And when two people understand each other in their
>   innermost hearts,
> Their words are sweet and strong, like the fragrance of orchids.

147

The Puer Eternus is the eternal youth inside us, innocent, tender, beautiful, yearning for guidance and protection. The Puer is a source of inspiration and sensual energy. In the past he has manifested as Dionysos the wine god, Hyacinthus beloved by Apollo, and Saint Sebastian with his arrows. In the unconscious, the Puer is forever attached to the source of the universe and all life, the ground and ocean of existence. Because of this, loving the Puer can lead to creativity. Many great philosophers and artists—Socrates, Leonardo da Vinci, and Oscar Wilde, for example— were inspired by this magical source, which helped them to create the beautiful things we remember them for today.

This happened through fantasy, when the artist saw a vision through the youth or youths he loved. Look at some of the Dialogues of Plato, for example, where Socrates sits down with a beautiful young man and talks about love as the doorway to spiritual realization. We know that Oscar Wilde was enraptured by handsome youths, the best known having been Lord Alfred Douglas. Many people might think that Wilde's love life was entirely separate and unconnected to his artistic genius, but I think the opposite was true: that Oscar Wilde's love life *was* an important source of his artistic inspiration. *The Picture of Dorian Gray*, for example, is about a Puer Eternus figure.

The point of what I'm saying is this—that your sex/love impulse can lead you to a powerful spirit world, which you can get in touch with by evoking the Double, in any of his forms, and following him into your inner reality. I believe whenever two men join closely, in sex, in love, in cuddling, even in a brief encounter between strangers, there is this mysterious power.

The reason we tend not to see this is because we're caught up in the mundane world of habits. We automatically assume the love-forces are *out there*, in another person, and not under our control. But if you try seeing that your fantasy images, ideals and desires are actually coming from *in you*, that you're creating them yourself, then you can open yourself to the inward call of the Double.

This is how we contain through our gay love great wonders and ways to grow. This is what I've found in myself by breaking the mirage of projections, of outside-sources: I see that the Double is a spirit, a daemon, an angel pointing the way to grow, showing me the sun path, the journey to the stars, to the wonderful, terrifying truths of my own being, my own god-hood. And if you look, I believe you'll find this to be true about yourself, too.

The Double leads us to another powerful spirit-source, the Anim. For men this is *the Anima*, the woman-essence within, the Great Mother, and those qualities and characteristics (that are non-sexist) called "feminine."

Through increased self-consciousness every man can realize his woman-essence; many gay men have already gone far in reaching their Anima, and expressing her, as can be seen in the popular gay worlds of drag and genderfuck.

The Anima, as "lady soul," as the Muses and Fates, is a powerful source of inspiration and understanding. In her guise as the Great Mother, she embodies wisdom and nurturance. The Great Mother is a name for that source in us of groundedness, like a great rooted tree, our connection to the land and to growing things in the land, to forests and animals, fields and crops, to birth and death. The Great Mother was a powerful god in many ancient cultures, where she was often portrayed as a statuesque woman with a thousand breasts, or as wearing a beard. In our society an awareness of the Great Mother survives in phrases like "Mother Earth" and "Mother Nature." In many cultures, gay men because of their Anima-sensitivity were often priests and shamans of the Great Mother god.

The Double and the Anim contain the non-sexist, pre-Patriarchal essences of what we call "masculine" and "feminine." When a person begins to realize they're both feminine and masculine, the spirit-forces lead to a beautiful realization, to the center-identity: androgyny. The Androgyne, who is neither a woman nor a man, but both, contains the powers of both. The Androgyne is the great harmonizer, source of visions, the gateway to the all-shining Point which the Hindus call Atman and the Christians call God. In the early Christian Coptic text of *The Gospel According to St. Thomas* Jesus says:

> When you make the two one, and when you make the inner as the outer, and when you make the male and the female into a single one, so that the male will not be male and the female not be female, when you make eyes in the place of an eye, and a hand in the place of a hand, and a foot in the place of a foot, and an image in the place of an image: then shall you enter the Kingdom!

Because of the essential equality basic to gay love (inherent in the Double), and because gay people are outcast from the society and its constricting consciousness, they have a spiritual potential for realizing the Androgyne within. This is a great gift and a burden, because with it comes a responsibility to help ourselves and humanity become more whole and harmonious. I've come to realize this as I've grown more and more aware of myself and other gay people. Feel within yourself: search for your magical spirit-source and open it. Go below the mundane surface of daily life and grasp your wonderful beauty.

I know that it's rough trying to be yourself in these days of mass production and consumption. So many people always seem to be telling us what to do. We've been conditioned since birth to wear blinders, and to believe in harmful fantasies like sex role and Romantic True Love. Society has tried to shape us into stunted, twisted images of ourselves.

But I think there's another voice that comes from inside us that also tells us what's good. Wasn't it from this inside source that we felt gay feelings, when everyone outside was saying how bad and wrong they were? For myself, I try to tune in on my inner self and block out this outside garbage, to become more myself. For me this is the good way to grow. I hope that in this book, I've suggested a few ways for you to become more yourself, too.

Notes

CHAPTER ONE: LOVING MEN, AN INTRODUCTION

"Homosexuality is as old . . .": quoted in A. Gide, *Corydon* (Farrar, Straus: N.Y., 1950), p. 113. *"Easily compared to the games . . .":* quoted in J. McCary, *Human Sexuality: Physiological and psychological factors of Sexual Behavior* (Van Nostrand Reinhold: N.Y., 1967), p. 160.

The following numbered footnotes refer to quotes in the text on pages 16–28:

1   H. Licht, *Sexual Life in Ancient Greece* (Barnes and Noble: N.Y., 1932), quoted in Churchill, p. 76. In addition, H. Ellis, *Studies in the Psychology of Sex* (Random House: N.Y., 1910) p. 9, notes that "the Egyptians showed great admiration of masculine beauty, and it would seem that they never regarded homosexuality as punishable or even reprehensible." Also, we find that the most ancient "civilized" peoples of the other "cradle of civilization," the Sumerians, have left us what appears to be their national poem, *The Epic of Gilgamesh* (see, for example, the translation by N. K. Sandars [Penguin: Baltimore, 1964. Paper.]), which is perhaps the oldest recorded heroic myth (third millennium B.C.). The theme is the gay love between the hero, Gilgamesh, and Enkidu his friend, and what befell them on their adventures.

2   Churchill, pp. 76–77. As examples of ancient pro-gay cultures, the author mentions the Celts, Greeks, Scandinavians, Egyptians, Etruscans, Cretans, Carthaginians, Sumerians, Canaanites, and Chaldeans.

3   G. R. Taylor, "Historical and Mythological Accounts of Homosexuality," in Marmor, pp. 140–164, pp. 149–150. Churchill, p. 75, adds that before the Exile the Jews "even accorded status to male temple prostitutes."

4   R. deBecker, *The Other Face of Love*, M. Crosland and A. Daventry, trans. (Grove: N.Y., 1969), p. 18.

5   Translation by W. H. D. Rouse (Mentor: N.Y., 1950. Paper.), p. 216.

6   Thucydides, *The Peloponnesian War*, R. Warner, trans. (Penguin: Baltimore, 1954. Paper.), pp. 399–403. Harmodius and Aristogiton became Greek national heroes to the cause of democracy, and were admired as models for the upbringing of young men. The Athenians held annual festivals to their memory, and they were often praised by poets and orators.

7   Aeschines, *Against Timarchus*, No. 49, 136–37, quoted in R. Flaceliere, *Love in Ancient Greece*, J. Cleugh, trans. (Crown: N.Y., 1962), p. 69.

8   W. Kayy, *The Gay Geniuses* (Marvin Miller: Glendale, Ca., 1965. Paper.), p. 28. To get an intimate feel for the depth and naturalness of gay feelings among men in Greek society, I suggest reading some of Mary Renault's marvelous historical novels, such as *The Last of the Wine, The Mask of Apollo,* and *The Persian Boy.* For a scholarly, yet readable, introduction to gay love in ancient Greece, I suggest Hans Licht's "Male Homosexuality in Ancient Greece," in D. Cory, *Homosexuality: A*

Cross-Cultural Approach (Julian: N.Y., 1956), pp. 267–349.

9   J. Mercer, *They Walk in Shadow* (Comet: N.Y., 1959), p. 27.

10   Quoted in F.-K. Forberg, *The Manual of Exotica Sexualia* (originally published as *Manuel d'Erotologie Classique,* 1882), (Brandon House: North Hollywood, Ca., 1965. Paper.), p. 90.

11   Distilled from the list provided by N. Garde, *Jonathan to Gide* (Vantage: N.Y., 1964), pp. 85–140 ff. I've listed emperors to suggest the extent of gayness in Roman culture. However, as innumerable graffiti uncovered in Pompeii show, it was quite common among all classes.

12   Karlen, pp. 38–39. The author also comments (pp. 35–37) that homosexuality was common (though illegal) in France from 1000 A.D. on. However, several Roman commentators (such as Athenaeus—see Forberg, p. 93) had noted homosexuality among the Gauls (early inhabitants of France) at a much earlier time.

13   Distilled from the list provided by Garde.

14   Karlen, p. 122.

15   Ellis, p. 32. Other famous artists of the Italian Renaissance who seemed to be gay include Michelangelo, of whom A. Symonds (*Life of Michelangelo,* 1895, vol. II) notes that he had "a notable enthusiasm for the beauty of young men . . . though he showed no partiality for women" (quoted in Ellis, pp. 32–33).

16   Quoted in H. M. Hyde, *The Love That Dared Not Speak Its Name* (Little, Brown: Boston, 1970), p. 42. The late sixteenth and seventeenth centuries produced a flourish of gay poetry in England. Examples include Richard Barnfield: "If it be sin to love a lovely lad, Oh, then sin I" (*The Affectionate Shepherd,* 1594); and John Wilmot, Earl of Rochester, who said in his *The Debauchee* (late 17th century):

> Then give me Health, Wealth, Mirth, and wine;
> And if busy love, intrenches,
> There's a sweet soft Page, of mine,
> Does the trick worth Forty Wenches.

17   Translation by A. Wainhous and R. Seaver (Grove: N.Y., 1966. Paper.), p. 232.

18   Garde, p. 14. Most of Anacreon's (ca. 572–488 B.C.) poetry has been lost, but fragments remain from the notes of others, such as this piece:

> I love Cleobulus
> I dote on Cleobulus
> I gaze at Cleobulus

19   Churchill, pp. 56–57. He goes on to add that "many of the famous cowboys and gunfighters would be considered homosexual by modern American standards. Billy the Kid, for example . . ."

20   From *Leaves of Grass.* The highest concenration of gay love feelings are in the "Calamus" and "Drum-taps" sections.

21   Quoted in Karlen, p. 253.

22   Kinsey *et.al.,* pp. 624–25.

23   Mercer, p. 27.

24   Quoted from his *Rare Adventures and Painefull Peregrinations* (MacLehose: Glasgow, 1906), in Karlen, p. 228.

25   This is from Richard Burton's translation (*The Book of the Thousand Nights and a Night* [The Burton Club: private edition, N.D.]). The *Nights* is peppered throughout with references to gay sex and love.

26   R. Surieu, *Sarv e' Naz, an essay on love and the representation of erotic themes in ancient Iran* (Nagel: Geneva, 1967), p. 170 and p. 172.

27   Translation by Surieu, p. 98. DeBecker notes (p. 65) "that practically all Moslem, Arab, or Persian poetry is tinged with homosexuality."

28   Burton, vol. 5, p. 156. I've included this comment as a warning that a great amount of censoring has been done for us in translations of written art, and that it's difficult to obtain honest copies of Persian, and for that matter, any written material praising gayness. I have seen the Hafiz poem (presented above) translated as: "Her curls in disarray, perspiring . . ." which makes a mockery of the poem and the artist, as well as our own culture.

29   A. Edwardes, *The Jewel in the Lotus* (Tandem: London, 1965. Paper.), p. 186. I recommend Edwardes' book for a delightfully intimate account of Middle Eastern sexual practices.

30   Recounted in Edwardes, pp. 193–94. According to Edwardes, gayness was particularly associated with religious sects, including the Druzes, Assassins, Janissaries, Hindee Thugs, the celibate hierarchy (*Sheykh-el-Islaum* and the *olemmah*) of the Moslem Church, and the Barmecides of Baghdad; also the Sufis, as Jami the poet tells us in a story: "There was a handsome boy who had wound the noose of desire round the neck of the dervishes, and had become, as it were, the point on the circle in the assembly of the Sufis . . ." (quoted in Surieu, p. 173).

31   Edwardes, p. 147; a private study by the author.

32   Edwardes, p. 172. The Bulgars, Tartars and Mongols are also mentioned by Ellis.

33   Edwardes, p. 181.

34   Paraphrasing Edwardes, p. 173. This was the same institution as existed among the ancient Greeks, especially the Spartans. The Thebans at one time had an elite corps of infantry called the "Sacred Band," composed entirely of pairs of lovers.

35   DeBecker, p. 76.

36   Quoted in Karlen, p. 229. A learned scholar from Taiwan, whom I knew at UCLA, once recounted an anecdote to me: she and a group of associates, during World War II, had gone to discuss a matter with the Chinese general of the northern front in Manchuria, who was staying on his private train. They came early in the morning, and were seated in a lounge just outside the bed chamber, to await the general's arousal. They waited and waited. My friend leaned over and asked her neighbor, who knew the general, in whispered tones, "Why does he take so long?" He whispered in reply, "He likes to relax while he can." So they waited. At last,

there was a stirring inside and the door opened. But out stepped a youth who shut the door and walked past the waiting visitors. "Who was that?" whispered my friend. "That's the general's boy," came the reply; "women are too much trouble to take on these war journeys."

37 DeBecker, p. 77. I once asked an elderly gentleman, visiting from China, what his fellow countrypeople thought of gay love. He replied that he was surprised we in this country made such a fuss about it, bad or good, since in China, he said, it was considered a part of the natural order of things.

38 Quoted in Karlen, p. 231.

39 DeBecker, p. 79. Karlen refers (p. 231) to this institutional gay love, while Edwardes speaks (p. 172) of the Samurai along with secret homosexual societies in Japan and China, and of male courtesans in Japan.

40 S. Ihara, *Comrade Loves of the Samurai*, E. Mathers, trans. (Charles Tuttle: Rutland, Vt., 1972. Paper.), p. 50.

41 Churchill, p. 78.
42 Ford and Beach, p. 130.

43 Ford and Beach, p. 130. Transvestites are found in many cultures throughout the world, such as the Chuckchee of Siberia, the Koniag of Alaska, the Lango of East Africa and the Tamala of Madagascar (Churchill, p. 81).

44 P. Gebhard, "Human Sexual Behavior: a Summary Statement," in D. Marshall and R. Suggs, *Human Sexual Behavior* (Basic: N.Y., 1971), pp. 206–217, pp. 214–215.

45 DeBecker, p. 6.

46 M. Eliade, *Shamanism*, W. Trask, trans. (Bollingen: N.Y., 1964), p. 351n and p. 258. Gay sexuality and shamanism were often connected in "primitive " societies.

47 W. B. Pomeroy, "Why We Tolerate Lesbians," *Sexology*, 31: 652–654, 1965, quoted in McCary, p. 283. Gayness was not restricted to Indian cultures occupying the area of the U.S., but extended to all the Americas, including such peoples as the Aztecs and Incas, Aymare of Bolivia, Gandavo of Brazil (see Karlen, p. 237) and so on. As an example, Karlen cites (p. 236) Cieza de Leon, Spanish chronicler of the Inca conquest:

> The Devill so farre prevayled in their beastly Devotions that there were Boyes Consecrated to serve in the Temple; and at the times of their Sacrifices and Solemne Feasts, the Lords and principall men abused them to that detestable filthinesse.

48 R. Benedict, *Patterns of Culture* (Houghton Mifflin: Cambridge, 1934), p. 263. Gay Indians were often considered specially skilled at certain tasks, and frequently played central roles in religious rites, as with the Mohaves, for example (see G. Devereaux, "Institutionalized Homosexuality of the Mohave Indians," in H. Ruitenbeek, *Homosexuality in Modern Society* [Dutton: N.Y., 1963]). See also M. Kenny, "Tinselled Bucks: An Historical Study in Indian Homosexuality," *Gay Sunshine*, No. 26/27, Winter 1975–76, pp. 16–17.

49 R. H. Denniston, "Ambisexuality in Animals," in J. Marmor, *Sexual Inversion* (Basic: N.Y., 1965), pp. 27–43, p. 42. Some scholars, such as A. Karlen, *Sexuality and Homosexuality* (Norton: N.Y., 1971), have tried to argue that such behavior seen in animal species is not homosexual but "displaced" behavior, that is, some other activity such as aggression transformed into a homosexual guise. Although it's true that in many "lower" species hormones etc. may be important, if we define "homosexual behavior" as sexual activity observed between same-sex animals (see A. Kinsey, W. Pomeroy, C. Martin, *Sexual Behavior in the Human Male* [Saunders: Philadelphia, 1948], p. 615), then these scholars' arguments are readily seen for what they are, specious attempts at heterosexual aggrandizement.

50 A. McBride and D. Hebb, "Behavior of the Captive Bottle-nose Dolphin, *Tursiops truncatus,*" *J. Comp. Physiol. Psychol.,* vol. XLI, pp. 111–123, 1948, p. 121.

Additional Notes from Chapter 1

"Gay people . . . have been struggling ever since oppression started . . .": A comprehensive history of the Gay Liberation Movement has yet to be prepared. But there are some good accounts of parts and aspects of it. James Steakley, *The Homosexual Emancipation Movement in Germany* (Arno: N.Y., 1975) covers in accurate detail the beginnings of organized Gay Rights and its political ups and downs. John Lauritsen and D. Thorstad have done a good job in their small book *The Early Homosexual Rights Movement (1864–1935)* (Times Change: N.Y., 1974. Paper). And J. Katz's two volumes *Gay American History* (1976) and *Gay/Lesbian Almanac* (1983) are especially invaluable. The best Gay Liberation anthologies are the two edited by Winston Leyland: *Gay Roots Vols. 1 & 2,* both with the subtitle *An Anthology of Gay History, Sex, Politics & Culture* (Gay Sunshine Press, 1991 & 1993). (The first of these vols. won the 1992 Lambda Book Award for best gay book by a gay press.) See also the two anthologies edited by Karla Jay/Allen Young: *Out of the Closets: Voices of Gay Liberation* (1972), and *After You're Out* (1975). Historical and literary works relating to individual gay persons are also important, such as those on the trials of Oscar Wilde and Roger Casement; also works by such writers as Gertrude Stein, Andre Gide (especially *Corydon,* a defense of gay love written in 1917), Robin Maugham, and many others. Gay Sunshine Press has published several literary collections, edited by Winston Leyland, among them: *Angels of the Lyre: A Gay Poetry Anthology* (1975), and *My Deep Dark Pain Is Love: A Collection of Latin American Gay Fiction* (1983); also by the same press the two pioneering volumes on Walt Whitman, *Calamus Lovers* (1987) and *Drum Beats* (1989), and the 1995 anthology *Tender Lads* on Russian gay literature. Lesbian books are numerous; among the early collections are Jill Johnston's *Lesbian Nation* (1973) and *The Lesbian Reader* (1975).

CHAPTER THREE: MASTURBATION

"*Masturbate, and then . . .*": quoted in A. Edwardes and R. Masters, *The Cradle of Erotica* (Matrix: N.Y., 1966), p. 227. "*Captive apes and monkeys . . .*": see Ford and Beach, p. 159. "*In one study young male chimpanzees . . .*": see *ibid.*, p. 135. "*With free living spider monkeys and baboons . . .*": see *ibid.*, p. 159 and p. 160. "*And elephants . . .*": see *ibid.*, p. 160. "*His excitement was evidenced . . .*": A. Shadle, "Copulation in the Porcupine," *J. Wildlife Management*, vol. X, pp. 1959–62, 1946, quoted in Ford and Beach, p. 160. "*Dolphins can be seen . . .*": see McBride and Hebb, cited in Ford and Beach, p. 160. "*Larger males will attempt . . .*": see Denniston, p. 41. "*This act is accomplished . . .*": F. Darling, *A Herd of Red Deer* (Oxford University: London, 1937), quoted in Ford and Beach, p. 161. "*Creates all living creatures . . .*": Edwardes and Masters, pp. 245–46. "*The Greeks and Romans thought . . . Mercury in Latin*": see Edwardes, p. 94. "*In most eastern cultures . . . at an early age*": see *ibid.*, pp. 95–96. "*Rubbing and constant handling . . .*": quoted in Edwardes and Masters, p. 239. "*Has become almost . . .*": quoted in *ibid.*, p. 231. "*Two scholars noted . . . ages of eleven and eighteen*": see *ibid.*, p. 230. "*Masturba-. tion was especially . . . you in the practice*": see *ibid.*, p. 280. "*Mutual or one-sided, as desired*": Ellis, p. 13. "*Felah the Negro . . .*": quoted in Edwardes and Masters, p. 86. "*Are not this child's eyes . . .*": *ibid.*, pp. 311–312. "*Masturbated by Agnee the Fire-Lord . . .*": Edwardes, p. 181. "*The favorite Hindoo youth . . .*": *ibid.*, p. 94. "*Was relished extensively*": *ibid.*, p. 95. "*Abuse their generative organs . . .*": Dr. Jacobus, *L'Ethnologie du Sens Genitale* (Paris, 1935), quoted in Edwardes and Masters, pp. 277–78. "*Having from infancy . . .*": Edwardes, p. 96. "*These include the Hopi . . . and Namu of Africa*": see Ford and Beach, p. 132. "*In certain Melanesian . . .*": see Karlen, pp. 480–81. "*In the Cubeo tribe . . .*": M. Opler, "Anthropological and Cross-Cultural Aspects of Homosexuality," in Marmor, pp. 108–123, pp. 116–117. "*Among the Tikopia . . .*": see Ford and Beach, p. 132. "*To some . . . but to others (and in some cultures) it's quite common*": especially as a method of rape, among the Mongols, Turks, and Muslims; see Edwardes and Masters, pp. 151–52.

CHAPTER FOUR: FELLATIO

"*The Muslims call them . . .*": quoted in Edwardes and Masters, p. 318. "*O Thaïs . . .*": translation by the author. "*This chapter is devoted . . . many others*": see G. Legman, *The Intimate Kiss* (Warner: N.Y., 1971. Paper.), pp. 178–179. I'm indebted to Legman for much of the material in this chapter. "*In the most natural manner . . . the arts of love*": Edwardes and Masters, p. 299. "*There are very old Egyptian pictures . . .*": see Ellis, p. 9. "*Through the middle . . .*": quoted in Forberg, p. 115. "*Why do you plague in vain . . .*": *ibid.* "*In Egypt, on the other . . .*": quoted in Edwardes and Masters, p. 298. "*Magnus Hirschfeld's pioneering research . . .*": cited in Karlen, p. 250. "*Among the Crow . . .*": Ford and Beach, p. 133. "*To the birth of Christ*": R. Burton and F. Arbuthnot, trans., *Kama Sutra of Vatsyayana*

(Putnam: N.Y., 1963. Paper.), p. 116. *"The male servants of some men . . ."*: Vat-syayana, *ibid.*, p. 118. *"Common and customary among all classes . . ."*: Edwardes and Masters, p. 299. *Fellatio allows greater variety . . ."*: Jacobus, *ibid.*, p. 310. *"The scene is the same all over . . ."*: Jacobus, *ibid.,* p. 318. *"The semen would appear . . ."*: quoted in A. Comfort, *The Joy of Sex* (Simon and Schuster: N.Y. 1972. Paper.), p. 130. *"In each and every case . . ."*: *The Gay Girl's Guide* (A Phallus Press Publication: Boston, 1949), quoted in Legman, p. 257.

CHAPTER FIVE: ANAL INTERCOURSE

"Buggery is no sinne": quoted in Hyde, p. 59. *"Aug. 7, 1911 . . ."*: quoted in Garde, p. 708. *"The Malekulians said . . ."*: J. Layard, *Stone Men of Malekula* (Chatto and Windus: London, 1942), quoted in Karlen, p. 482. *"Was accompanied by frequent sodomy . . ."*: G. Hamilton, "A Study of Sexual Tendencies in Monkeys and Baboons," *J. Anim. Behav.*, vol. IV, pp. 295-318, 1914, quoted in Ford and Beach, p. 135. *"As noticed in squirrel monkeys"*: see Denniston, p. 41. *"Among that unusually complex animal the porpoise . . ."*: see McBride and Hebb, cited in Ford and Beach, p. 139. *"Held to be pure . . . and holy"*: Edwardes, p. 159. *"The Egyptians Set and Horus"*: see deBecker, pp. 14–15. *"Quite common if not customary"*: Edwardes and Masters, p. 218. *"Although most modern scholars now think Sodom was . . ."*: see S. Gearhart and W. Johnson, *Loving Women/Loving Men, Gay Liberation and the Church* (Glide: San Francisco, 1974. Paper.), pp. 30 ff. *"By Paiderastia a man propagated his virtues . . ."*: Ellis, p. 12. *"Lycurgus, a Spartan . . ."*: Forberg, p. 85. *"Who does not know . . ."*: after Aloysia Sigaea, by Forberg, p. 78. *"A man who exercises . . ."*: Forberg, pp. 45–46. *"Stretch the foot . . ."*: *ibid.*, p. 71. *"Caesar, the husband . . ."*: *ibid.*, p. 80. *"Catching me with a boy . . ."*: *ibid.*, p. 89. *"He was very much given . . ."*: *ibid.*, p. 56. *"For you, ungrateful boy . . ."*: *ibid.*, p. 97. *"It is not considered objectionable . . ."*: quoted in Churchill, p. 77, from the translation by Licht. *"The Celts take more pleasure . . ."*: quoted in Forberg, p. 93. *"Among the Normans"*: see Karlen, p. 86. *"This sin has been so public . . ."*: in Migne, *Patrologie*, vol. CLIX, col. 95, quoted in Ellis, p. 40. *"For beastly Sodomy . . ."*: quoted in Taylor, p. 141. *"If we may trust to Aloysia Sigaea . . ."*: Forberg, p. 94. *"Including one of the most ancient . . ."*: Edwardes, p. 158. *"Thus sodomy was connected with . . ."*: see *ibid.*, p. 194. *"Facing Mecca . . ."*: translated by Erskine Lane, in *Gay Sunshine Anthology* (Gay Sunshine Press: San Francisco, 1977). *"When he had undone the cord . . ."*: quoted in Surieu, pp. 127–28. *"The penis smooth and round . . ."*: quoted in Edwardes and Masters, p. 197. *"The worth of slit . . ."*: quoted in Edwardes, p. 175. *"The epithet el-fa'eel . . ."*: *ibid.*, p. 163. *"Is not only frequent . . ."*: R. Bey, *Darkest Orient* (Arco: London, 1953), quoted in Edwardes and Masters, pp. 280–81. *"My prickle is big . . ."*: quoted in Edwardes and Masters, p. 282. *"As dancing boys they . . ."*: Edwardes, pp. 188–189. *"When King Richard . . ."*: Edwardes and Masters, p. 218. *"Also with the Berbers, Moors . . ."*: see Edwardes, p. 167. *"May the devil . . ."*: *ibid.*, p. 175. *"There's a boy across the river . . ."*: Edwardes and Masters, p.

200. *"Except that it was at least fairly popular"*: see Edwardes, p. 181. *"Flagrant sodomy"*: ibid., p. 172. *"The Elizabethan Samuel Purchas"*: quoted in Karlen, p. 228. *"Duke Ling . . ."*: E. Chow, *The Dragon and the Phoenix* (Arbor House: N.Y., 1971), p. 19. *"During the Manchu dynasty"*: ibid., pp. 90–92. *"Hsi-men opened the boy's robe . . ."*: quoted in Edwardes and Masters, p. 222. *"A thriving and honorable profession"*: Edwardes, p. 191. *"The boys were made . . ."*: deBecker, p. 78. *"Anal coitus is the usual . . ."*: Gebhard, p. 215. *"Such customs have been noted among . . ."*: see deBecker, pp. 16–19. *"The last which was taken . . ."*: quoted in Burton, "Terminal Essay," p. 244. *"Among many of the aborigines . . ."*: Ford and Beach, p. 132, with reference to C. Strehlow, "Die Aranda- und Loritja-Stämme in Zentral-Australien," Pt. 4, "Das Soziale Leben der Aranda und Loritja." *Veröffentlichungen aus dem Städtischen Völker-Museum*, Vol. I, pt. 4, sec. 1, pp. 1–103, sec. 2, pp. 1–78 (Joseph Baer: Frankfurt am Main, 1915), p. 98. *"Keraki bachelors . . ."*: ibid., p. 132. *"Among the Siwans . . ."*: ibid.

CHAPTER SIX: S & M AND OTHER SCENES

"Stephen and Michael . . .": James Mitchell, "The Orgy," W. Leyland, ed., *Angels of the Lyre* (1975). *"For gay males the appeal . . ."*: "Mitzel's Ten Points in Criticism of the Current Vogue of Today's L & L/S & M/F-F Scene Among Homosexuals," *Fag Rag*, No. 14, Nov./Dec. 1975, p. 21; see also "S & M and Gay Lib" by Craig Hanson, *Gay Sunshine*, No. 14, Aug. 1972, p. 7 and p. 14; in contrast to these two critical articles, see "Inside S & M" by Ian Young, *Gay Sunshine*, No. 25, Summer 1975, pp. 8–9.

CHAPTER SEVEN: LOVE AND GAY CONSCIOUSNESS

"It was in the night . . . ": J. Conrad, "The Secret Sharer," *A Conrad Argosy* (Doubleday, Doran: Garden City, 1942), pp. 269–92, p. 274. *"My brother Jonathan . . . "*: II Samuel I: 26. *"But when two people . . . "*: quoted in R. Wilhelm, *The I Ching or Book of Changes*, C. Baynes, trans. (Harper: N.Y., 1950), vol. 1, p. 329. *"In many cultures, gay men . . . "*: see E. Carpenter, *Intermediate Types Among Primitive Folk* (Arno: N.Y., 1975), p. 31; and also deBecker, p. 86. For an introduction to the relations between Jungian archetypes and gay love, see M. Walker, "The Double, an Archetypal Configuration," *Spring, an Annual of Archetypal Psychology and Jungian Thought* (Spring Publications: N.Y., 1976).

BOOKS FROM LEYLAND PUBLICATIONS / G.S PRESS